faith

made

visible

faith

made

visible

shaping the human spirit in sculpture and word

Text and sculptures by

Charles McCollough

Poetry by

Maren Tirabassi

United Church Press

Cleveland, Ohio

United Church Press, Cleveland, Ohio 44115
Text and sculptures © 2000 by Charles McCollough
Poetry © 2000 by Maren C. Tirabassi
Spanish translations of poetry by Esther Rendon-Portillo

Quote from Doug Purnell, *Painting the Way: Addressing and Equipping the
Imagination in Theological Education* (Chalice Press, forthcoming), used by permission
of the author. • All sculpture photographs are by Robert P. Matthews and
Sara G. Matthews, SGM Photography, Princeton, N.J., and are used by permission.

05   04   03   02   01   00   5   4   3   2   1

Library of Congress Cataloging-in-Publication Data

McCollough, Charles R., 1934–
    Faith made visible: shaping the human spirit in sculpture and word/text and sculptures
    by Charles McCollough ; poetry by Maren Tirabassi.
        p.   cm.
    ISBN 0-8298-1378-0 (pbk. : alk. paper)
    1. Christianity and the arts.   2. Christian poetry, American.   I. Tirabassi, Maren C.
    II. Title.

BR115.A8 M38 2000
246—dc21   00-023465

"Rejoice that faith has brought us home to sight."

—St. Augustine, *On the Trinity*

CONTENTS

LIST OF SCULPTURES AND POEMS

Sculpture	Poem
23. *Reclining Woman*	"Maybe"
24. *Anger*	"Anger"
25. *Old Fighter*	"The Old Fighter"
26. *Valerie*	"Valerie"
27. *Search*	"Search"
28. *Twisted Man*	"Twisted Man and Twisted Woman"
29. *Twisted Woman*	"Twisted Man and Twisted Woman"
30. *Nun*	"A Small Remembering"
31. *Orpheus*	"Orpheus"
32. *Orpheus and Eurydice*	"Orpheus and Eurydice"
33. *Unfinished Madonna*	"Unfinished Madonna"
34. *Eve*	"Eve"
35. *Escape-Women*	"Escape-Women"
36. *Just Peace Award*	"Just Peace Award"
37. *Crucifixion*	"Terra-cotta Crucifix"
38. *Joy*	"Ode to Joy"
39. *Candle Holders*	"Phalanges Candelabra"
40. *Jesus and Children*	"New Translation"
41. *Crucifix*	

ACKNOWLEDGMENTS

I can name only a few of the people who indulged my passion for art, taught and encouraged me over the years. Professors Carl Michalson and Jane Dillenberger inspired me to see beyond words at Drew Graduate School of Theology. Art historian Allison Hardwick took me to my first art class when I was twenty-nine and choking with words. Sculptors John Carbone and Jim Colavita showed me the mysteries of clay over many years of sculpture classes. Hebrew Bible scholar Hugh White helped me understand how Scripture affirms even graven images. Writers Shirley and Rudy Nelson advised me to write a right-brain book, personal and visual.

The Office for Church in Society of the United Church of Christ and its director, Wallace Ryan Kuroiwa, kept me working for social justice and sculpting too. Theologian Douglas Meeks and artist Catherine Kapikian opened many doors for me at Wesley and beyond. Doug Purnell, fellow artist-in-residence at Wesley, taught me to hope for the visual arts in the church. Poet Maren Tirabassi has helped me connect words and images through her brilliant poetry. Potter Ursala Kaplowitz patiently fired many of my ceramic pieces. My local church, Christ Congregation, and pastor Jeffrey Mays often showed my work there. Photographers Sara and Robert Matthews gracefully and professionally shot the photos.

My family has been the most tolerant and supportive. My brother, architect George McCollough, always encourages me. My children, Colin, Wendy, and Tim, are able models and ready critics. Most of all, even before this journey began and through it all, my wife, Carol, made it possible, and to her I dedicate this book.

Faith and Grace, Art and Awe

My family doctor warned me that I might have cancer. I had a test showing warning signs. He recommended I go to a urologist whose specialty includes prostate cancer. I did, and that doctor recommended an ultrasound test and biopsy. This all took months of getting on doctors' schedules and arranging for insurance coverage. I used the time to study what prostate cancer was and to worry. As I read about it and looked at pictures of its victims in their last days, I really got scared.

I have three friends with cancer, and we discussed it often. The worry rarely left my mind as the tests and monitoring dragged on over two years. I went through the very painful ultrasound test and biopsy and waited for results. The urologist took his time and eventually concluded that the biopsy was "inconclusive." I thought, "This is ridiculous. After you carved twelve samples of tissue out of me, you can't conclude anything?" He recommended I go through this again if the next blood test showed the need. My fear turned to a chronic ache in my soul. There were no painful symptoms, but the worry began to wear me down. My life became dull and frightful. I pictured myself as skin and bones dying a slow, miserable death. Although I went about my daily life as usual on some levels, deep down I started preparing for shutting down my future and saying goodbye to all I loved.

I took the blood test again in six months. It was worse. A second ultrasound test and a biopsy were ordered. But this time I asked my family doctor to recommend another specialist. He did, and I went into his office like a "dead man walking."

After waiting for test results, I finally sat down with him to go over the ultrasound test and biopsy report. He showed me the pictures and said, "You do not have cancer." It is a great understatement to say that his words and the pictures of the healthy glans were good news. Such words are inadequate to my feelings of relief and joy. It is more accurate to say I had been given a new life. I had been redeemed from death. I had been reborn to begin a new future without this terrible threat hanging over me. On my drive home from the doctor's office, I thought of the mountains and hills bursting forth in singing and the trees clapping their hands (Isaiah 55:12). I warned myself to try to act normal and not have a wreck. I said, "Thank you, God. I owe you one. I owe you many. I owe you my life."[1]

I consider this experience to be a salvation moment and the doctor's words and pictures to be not only good news; they were my gospel at that moment. I mean this quite literally. I do not mean it figuratively or in a secondary sense in which salvation or being born again really happens only at a church revival or in prayer with a pastor and that this doctor's words and pictures were *like* that. No, I mean that when the doctor said, "You do not have cancer," and verified it with the ultrasound picture, that was God's gospel to me, and I was saved then and there, born again to new life. There was no residual truth or ritual I had to find or practice. That good news was complete, requiring no doctrine, theology, or spiritual discipline to sanctify it.

This raw experience of my rebirth was a spiritual event. There was no physical illness. Such experiences have happened at other times in small ways. They are occasions of unexpected reprieve,[2] and I have found that each experience is followed by pure joy in which I see, hear, smell, taste, feel, sense, and act as though God's creation is good beyond all measure; and I am flooded with delight at the smallest things. The colors of flowers are brighter, the sky is bluer, the music of wind in the trees sings for joy, and even crabby people are more tolerable. "The world is charged with the grandeur of God," as Gerard Manley Hopkins proclaims in his poem "God's Grandeur."

I believe that such moments of unexpected reprieve are what is meant by the word "grace" and that my joyful response to such reprieves is the meaning of the word "faith." Such moments also compel me to new behavior with more acts of kindness and a greater sense of urgency for making the world better for others.

Two simple but important issues arise from these moments of reprieve and joy that frame the direction of this book: first, *how can we keep such joy in our lives?* Cancer and an endless list of other evils are real and may afflict me or anyone at any time. All too quickly, the daily grind sets in. Even on the way home from the doctor's office, a tailgater took his place at my rear bumper and communicated his "road rage" with the minimal subtlety of his horn. Some of my rages from my past quickly flared up to dull and blind my joy and delight. Even before I reached home and told my wife the good news, I was tempted to slide back into the old ruts and habits and daily patterns of survival. But the joy was too strong for me to worry about a tailgater. I slowed down even more and waved at him a happy greeting.

The second issue is, *how can we communicate such good news to others?* I am clear that such experiences of new life and rebirth precede all the language, images, and actions we use to describe such experiences. This may seem obvious, but it is often ignored in religious communication. To insist that others "believe" in a gospel or in God or Jesus or Buddha or Muhammad or, much less, in a nation or flag has limited value to me and can even be dangerous. Rather, I believe that spiritual communication works the other way around. The experience precedes the words, images, and acts. So the best way to share our joy and good news is to live them in our deeds and to communicate in words and images that help others name their own salvation experiences. By contrast, to encourage others to cite religious sentences might force them to some kind of mental assent, but it does not cause authentic change. Such salvation events must come from within, not without. Just as no woman can be fully tuned to my fears of prostate cancer, as a male, I can never really know a woman's pain of cervical cancer. But with words, images, and actions that connect to others' real-life experience (as distinct from correct statements and propositions), we can begin to share profoundly this joy of good news.

Assuming that the experience precedes the verbal, visual, and behavioral representation of it is the first step to keeping and sharing the good news. But the matter is much deeper, so much so that a whole philosophical and theological movement called "existentialism" relentlessly proclaimed the point with the phrase "existence precedes essence." The task of this book is to present in images and poetry a way to reach more effectively the raw experiences we have from which deeds, images, and words come. I will call what we are up to simply "visual communication." I want not only to *say* but also to *show* how visual communication, particularly sculpture, poetry, and social action are essential to sharing the joy of unexpected reprieves.

I have another personal story to tell. Contrary to the task of this book, I have spent most of my life deeply committed to and professionally occupied in verbal and written communication. I began daily journal writing years ago and never go a day without writing an entry. After college I spent seven years of full-time study for a degree to teach theology and philosophy in college. It was a rigorous discipline involving the most abstract concepts and the fewest possible visual helps to learning. I began theological study with a professor who attracted the most academically inclined students to his classes because of his stern demands and tough grading. The attraction seems to have been that if you could pass his course in philosophical theology, you could do anything. I subscribed to this theory at the time but would have much preferred to study with a professor who taught literature and the arts. Yet I believed then that such a preferred course of study would weaken my determination to press on for the advanced degree and eventually to earn a living as a college teacher of theology. But one day I overheard the stern professor exclaim that the other teacher "had all the fun" teaching literature and the arts. It was an off-the-cuff remark, but it rang true to me at a deep level. Literature and art were more fun. But there was no way I could see practically to go in this direction. I knew of no jobs in this field.

I have always drawn pictures and studied art books informally. I drew caricatures of my teachers, and I developed a way of graphically charting abstract ideas so I could understand them in spatial relationships. But these efforts were untutored. I had never taken an art course, that is, not until my last year of graduate school. I was struggling through a number of heavy courses including one on Immanuel Kant's *Critique of Pure Reason,* and I was lost. Then a friend invited me to take an evening class in drawing. I went. I loved it and have continued such night courses ever since. I got through the course on Kant but only after making a graphic chart of the whole book on a large piece of butcher paper.

Studying, writing, and lecturing on philosophy and theology are critical tasks. I am sure of that, and I do not regret any of my work in this area. But it is hard work for me. I developed a routine of working at this in the daytime and playing at art in the evenings. Also in the last year of my graduate studies, I attended a slide lecture of an art historian, Jane Dillenberger, who was well known for her enchanting slide presentations. I was enchanted. But as before, I saw no way I could make a living in art, and by then my wife was pregnant and I would soon have to do honest labor every day.

I worked for many years as pastor, teacher, and activist, and I could play at art only at night and on vacations. But I continued working in art, particularly sculpture, anytime I could. Because my jobs have involved considerable travel, I could not carry clay easily. So I sketched in pencil and ink and went to every art museum and gallery I could find in the cities of my travels.

While viewing or sketching the masters of visual art or working in clay, I often feel joy and delight. In the presence of artistic genius it is easy to feel awe and wonder. Over these years I never considered myself an artist; I only admired the masters and enjoyed sculpting as my recreation. Sometimes after I had escaped work to go to an art museum or gallery, my enchantment would carry over for a while afterward. I would see a tree or a person as Van Gogh or Rodin might represent it. The joy would carry over into my life at least for a short time, but would soon fade into the ordinary daily routine.

Finally, an amazing connection came to me. The joy I felt before a great work of art, the joy I felt in moments when I shaped clay in an especially expressive way, and the joy of experiences of unexpected reprieve were all the same joy. When I experienced reprieve from cancer, I felt the same enchantment with all life as when I was in a highly creative period and when I was under the spell of a genius work of art. At these times I would see, hear, smell, taste, feel, and sense the wonder of God's creation as if I were the first person on earth. The joy and wonder of unexpected reprieve, cre-

ativity, and enchantment are all the same thing for me now. Seeing great art and espe-
cially creating sculpture give me this joy.

It took many years to discover this connection. It was slow in coming because I am
a theologian whose language is the written/spoken word, and such a connection is
beyond the fringe of orthodox theology. My days of work and nights of art were sep-
arate worlds. For years I regarded my playing with clay as my "dirty little secret." I even
felt guilty about doing it. Did not the King James Version and the Revised Standard
Version command us to make no graven image (Exodus 20:4; Leviticus 19:4; Deuteron-
omy 4:16–18; 5:8)? I knew of no one, with the exception of the part-time teachers I
mentioned and Paul Tillich, who seriously connected theology and the visual arts. Still,
Tillich was a theologian, not an artist. These disciplines stand in separate worlds and
almost never touch. Generally, the disdain most artists hold for theology is matched only
by the disuse most theologians (at least Protestant theologians) have for the arts. This is
sadly the case even though theology and art are about the deepest dimensions of real-
ity, which is the source of both, according to Tillich.

When these fields of art, poetry, and theology are joined with actions for justice and
peace, the oddity becomes curious indeed. Yet that is where my journey has led me,
and it is what I seek to express in this book with the poet Maren Tirabassi, with whom
I share these curious connections.

I will finish this chapter with another story that is not personal. Among other social
actions, Maren and I have worked to get our government to sign the international treaty
banning landmines. A part of this effort has been a poem and sculpture that have been
used in this campaign. (See figure 1, *Landmines*, page 34.) But little of this compares to
the work of Bobby Muller, who headed the International Campaign to Ban Landmines
that won the 1997 Nobel Peace Prize.

A wounded Vietnam War veteran and a paraplegic, Muller organized the Vietnam
Veterans of America Foundation. This organization led many others in an amazingly
successful effort to ban these grisly weapons that kill and maim twenty-six thousand
people every year, mostly civilians and often children. The International Campaign,
along with its American coordinator, Jody Williams, won the Nobel Peace Prize after
six years of tough organizing. Getting this treaty signed by 150 nations is truly a mirac-
ulous feat.

Muller was wounded not by a landmine but by gunfire in Vietnam. Yet a visit to
Cambodia after the war convinced him of the urgency of banning these insidious
weapons as he saw countless civilians being indiscriminately maimed by mines still
buried years after the war was over. He stayed in the background during the Nobel
award ceremonies, but in a *New York Times* article he said about his own near-death
experience in Vietnam that he was "convinced I . . . was going to die. [But] I woke up
alive. . . . My reaction was one of absolute, complete ecstasy. Instead of cashing in my
chips, I was going back to play the game again."[3]

Muller seems to keep this ecstasy of his unexpected reprieve alive and share it with others by tenaciously fighting to rid the world of landmines. Yet does it take great trauma to motivate such good work? It seems so for most of us. Are there other ways than near-death trauma to initiate the joy and ecstasy of life?

I think we start by making these curious connections of faith, art, and social justice. But this is not so curious when we begin with the raw experience of life rather than with the congealed language about it found in orthodox texts. Then we see that all such words, images, and actions are attempts to express the meaning of these experiences rather than the reverse (that is, rather than trying to make saving experiences happen with correct words, images, and actions). And we see that such salvation moments need not only words but also images and actions to make them last and to make them translate most effectively to others. This is what we hope to communicate in the visual language of poetry and the visual images of sculpture as we focus them on the spiritual, moral, and political issues of our time. If we assume that experience precedes language, image, and act, that assumption relativizes all communication forms (verbal, visual, literary, scientific, theological, etc.) and allows all forms of expression access to our initial, raw experience. All forms can contribute to truth free from a hierarchy of truth that rigidly compartmentalizes and isolates fields of inquiry and pits them one against the other. Rather, with this assumption that experience precedes expressions of it, the boundaries between fields of knowledge come down. The boundaries between the "hard" sciences and the "soft" humanities and the arts even fall. Every field with its special form of expression seeks to make sense of raw experience, and we need them all. The language of the arts is as valuable as that of science.

If we are to make the moments of joy and delight last for ourselves and connect to others, it helps to believe that these moments, even as ephemeral as they are, are nevertheless what creation is meant to be.[4]

The Visual Gospel

The first church I served as full-time minister was founded in 1717 in New England. It was painted white inside and out. The walls, the pulpit, the ceiling, the altar, and the steeple were all white. The clapboard siding was repainted white every few years. The church was so white that townsfolk simply called it "the White Church." I never heard a member object to this nickname, and I even detected a sense of pride in its plain whiteness. There were no diversions of color, painting, sculpture, or imagery to distract the congregation from the Word that was read, preached, and sung.

One compromise had been allowed some years before my arrival. A golden cross was placed on the altar. I was aware of the history of the early Congregational Church that broke from the Church of England and determined to purify itself of all images. It followed literally the words in the King James Version: "Thou shalt not make unto thee any graven image" (Exodus 20:4; see also Leviticus 19:4; Deuteronomy 4:16–18; 5:8). Such images smacked of idolatry and the worship of saints, which we Protestants had long protested. Since basically the same translation appeared in the Revised Standard Version in 1952 ("You shall not make for yourself a graven image"), I wondered how the image of the cross got into the White Church. So I asked a deacon of the church. He did not want to say much about it, other than it had caused a church fight.

The cross of gold group obviously won the fight, but negative feelings seemed to remain. A golden cross felt too close to a golden calf, which in the Hebrew Bible was roundly condemned by Moses as idolatry. I sensed that it would not take much for a "Moses" or two on the Board of Deacons to condemn this cross on the altar of the White Church and remove it so that the plain whiteness would reign unchallenged by any color or image.

I could understand this attempt to focus on reading, writing, speaking, singing, and hearing the Word without visual distractions. Some of the sentimental pictures in church school materials and in the dusty cathedrals of Europe were painful to view. But the major problem with visual communication in Christian churches was that the second of the Ten Commandments explicitly forbids making graven images. This is forbidden not only in much of Protestant Christianity, but in Judaism and Islam as well. For we all share allegiance to these Commandments. Consequently, many but not all Jews and Muslims limit the placing of images in synagogues and mosques to avoid figurative imagery. Hebrew tradition stresses the word, and music and dance are highly developed. In Islam elaborate graphic designs have emerged as a special art form but usually without representational images.

Many Protestant groups took up this practice after the sixteenth century because it fit their reaction against the Roman Catholic competitive patronage of the visual arts. Some radical Protestants even destroyed the visual arts in churches. All Protestants affirmed the phrase *sola scriptura*. Scripture *alone* was the *sole* authority for them.

Although I appreciated the desire to avoid distracting images, I still loved the visual arts. But how could I pursue them when so much in the Bible and tradition seemed to forbid such art, especially in holy places? How could I practice my art when I was teaching the Ten Commandments to confirmation classes at the same time? I was taking art classes at night while during the day I was collecting a salary from the White Church that prided itself on its plainness without color or images. At best, I felt torn; at worst, hypocritical. Nevertheless, for many years I divided my life between the verbal and the visual and kept them apart, feeling a twinge of guilt at my night life of forbidden visual delights.

I lived a long time with this major contradiction, and though I have never been a literalist, I searched the Scriptures on and off to find relief from this division in my life. Reading the letters in the Christian Scriptures was no help on this issue. In 1 Corinthians 12:8–10, Paul listed the gifts of the Spirit, such as utterances of wisdom and knowledge, prophecy, and speaking in tongues. Not a single one of them is related to the visual arts. Likewise in Ephesians 4:11–12, we learn of the gifts from Christ: people would be "apostles, some prophets, some evangelists, some pastors and teachers, to equip the saints for the work of ministry." There is not a word about artists.

Yet I continued my nocturnal study of sculpture and drawing, ignoring my other commitments to scriptural authority. Then one day, after years of presumed defiance of the Second Commandment, I read an article about Bezalel, a Bible character I had over-looked. Bezalel was filled with the Spirit of God and with ability, intelligence, knowledge, and craft. He was told to "devise artistic designs"[1] in gold, silver, bronze, stone, and wood for the tent of meeting. I could not quite believe what I read and quickly grabbed a Bible and turned to Exodus 31. There it was! God commanded an artist through Moses to make visual art for the worship center. They were artworks of all kinds: vestments, furniture, and utensils to adorn the tent of meeting. How could this be? Only eleven chapters after the commandment to make no graven image, God told Bezalel through Moses to make graven images. What is going on here?

Then I noted that the command to make visual art was given *before* the story of the children of Israel making and falling down to worship the idol of the golden calf in Exodus 32. Surely, this abuse of image making would be forbidden after the Hebrews had learned this lesson. So much for the hope that somewhere in Scripture it would say that image making and the arts were at least acceptable, if not blessed, activities.

I am glad I kept reading. I found something I had never seen before. After the dust had settled, Moses had killed some of the idolaters, and God's anger at the worship of the golden calf idol had been appeased, the commissioning of Bezalel was repeated. In Exodus 35 and 36, Bezalel was once again inspired to "devise artistic designs" for the tent of meeting in gold, silver, bronze, stone, and wood. That was after the golden calf was destroyed and the people were punished for their idolatry. Something is strange here. Clearly, there has to be a difference between worshiping idols and making visual artistic images. On the one hand, making art is not only affirmed but also ordered by God; yet on the other hand, worship of the golden calf idol is condemned.

We still have the Second Commandment clearly stating in the Revised Standard Version (RSV), "You shall not make for yourself a graven image." And we have centuries of traditions that take these words literally in three major religions of the world.

In 1989 a new translation of the Bible, the New Revised Standard Version (NRSV), was published. The slight change of just one word from the RSV makes an astonishing difference. Instead of translating Exodus 20:4 as, "You shall not make for yourself a graven image," the NRSV translates the passage, "You shall not make for yourself an idol."[2] To make no "idol" rather than make no "image" thus made the Second Commandment consistent with the distinction in Exodus 31 and 35 between image making (Bezalel's calling) and idol making (golden calf worship) so firmly forbidden.[3]

It is hard to overstate the importance of this new translation for visual art after centuries of interpretations that equated image making with idol making. My personal response to this discovery was to feel as if a heavy burden had been lifted. Finally, I could bring my sculpture in out of the dark. Image making was not only acceptable but *assigned* to a visual artist, Bezalel. Just like the prophets and other holy persons, he was filled with the Spirit of God. To be sure, even without this translation, the Roman Catholic and Eastern Orthodox and most Episcopal and Lutheran Churches had patronized visual arts throughout Western history. Such imagery was essential for fifteen hundred years to communicate the Christian message because very few people were literate. Painting, sculpture, architecture, and stained glass told the story of Jesus again and again in images that illiterate people could "read" in these churches.

Thank goodness for this patronage! Without it we would not have many of the masterworks of Western art. Michelangelo would not have carved the *Pietà* or painted the Sistine Chapel.

After decades of quiet study of sculpture and drawing, I began to exhibit my work in galleries, churches, and seminaries. The sky did not fall. I was not punished with Moses' avenging sword. Gradually, all guilt dissolved. Perhaps like the art of Bezalel, my art could be a way of expressing the good news of God's love, a visual gospel. I was convinced long ago that *seeing* things of beauty in God's creation evoked joy in me. I assumed it happened in others. I knew that I never even began fully to see common trees, flowers, or people until I started the deep study of their features, shades of color, gestures, and shadows as I drew or sculpted them. Image making helps me to see the uniqueness, mystery, and ultimately, God's sacredness revealed through these subjects of my art.

Now I could focus on art as well as writing and speaking without any restraint other than my time, energy, and ability. Lifting the burden of contradiction also lifted the scales from my eyes. I could understand things differently. I grasped new insights in Scripture. For example, it is well known that when Jesus taught his disciples, their ears and hearing were opened to hear the good news. It is usually assumed that such new hearing of God's Word was a spiritual change, not only an end to physical deafness. Yet when we read about Jesus healing a blind person (for example, Bartimaeus; Mark 10:46–52) or "recovery of sight to the blind" (Luke 4:18) or Paul's regaining his sight (Acts 9:18), we more often limit the interpretation of these healings to physical miracles that overshadow the spiritual vision given by Jesus. But believing in the goodness and grace of God opens our eyes to see the beauty of a sunset or starry night anew as well as to hear freshly the music of birds singing or Mozart's *Requiem*. I began to understand how living my life in a state of unexpected reprieve or grace helped me to see more vividly the rich textures and the infinite variety of life. I could see how Jesus offered not only saving words but also saving images and vision.

I also began to notice that we in the iconoclastic traditions have denied ourselves a full half of our minds to the enterprise of communicating this good news. Even though Jesus summed up the commandments of God in the Great Commandment (Matthew 22:36–38) calling us to love God with all our hearts, souls, and minds, we have neglected the full use of our minds. The visual/spatial functions occur in the whole right hemisphere of our minds. By avoiding images and subordinating art, we have left the right hemisphere of the mind dormant, focusing almost exclusively on reading, writing, and speaking words—all functions of the left hemisphere of the mind. But the Great Commandment still stands, urging us to use all our minds to love God.

One exhibit of my sculpture and Maren's poetry was held at a seminary near Boston. For the opening we gave a slide lecture and invited all our friends from the Boston area. I made a special effort to invite a prominent pastor, who was a friend. I went to his study and sat down to exchange news of common friends and to get reacquainted. He was friendly and gracious. But when I invited him to the exhibit opening, he turned angry and made a speech about how visual art had been one of the major problems of Christian history. I was stunned by this attitude from someone I otherwise highly respected. I struggled without success to respond and left his study saddened and amazed at his reaction to my invitation.

As usual my good arguments come long after I need them. I could understand his opinion because there are risks and dangers in the use of images. But they are no more or less than the risks and dangers in the use of words. It is so easy to turn things of beauty and art into obsessions or idols that the Bible frequently warns us against. We do not worship golden calves anymore, but we still create and worship idols of beauty and obsessive images of wealth and power. These images are easily manipulated by advertising to enslave us to debt and to any power that promises us the fulfillment of false riches. Images can be exploited with great demonic power to both attract and repel us. The gods have always fascinated and terrified us, as Rudolf Otto showed in his 1923 book *The Idea of the Holy*. But my pastor friend did not seem to be aware that words can be as demonic and idolatrous as images. There are demonic words as well as demonic images that attract and repel us obsessively.

For example, there are words such as curses, obscenities, stereotypical labeling, bigoted jokes, and slanderous gossip that seek to tear down other people. There are evil words too shameful to print. News reports and scandal journalism, however, continue shamelessly to spread offensive words and gossip in order to sell their stories and to attract advertisers.

Euphemistic words are used to cover violent and demonic acts. For example, the military claims to inflict "collateral damage," meaning that civilians were killed. And there are seductive, enchanting words, such as, "You can have all the food you desire, miracles in your hands, and all the power you want to rule others" (Matthew 4:1–10). These demonic words were offered to Jesus as he fasted in the wilderness. But we hear such words daily tempting us to claim we are superior or inferior, a "master race" or a "pitiable worm." There is no end to the abuse of words or images. Both can be dangerous or edifying, demeaning or uplifting. The Second Commandment warns us not to make idols out of images; the Third Commandment warns us not to misuse words about God; the Ninth Commandment warns us not to make false witness, or lies out of words. But no one suggests that we stop using words because the evil of cursing and telling lies is so tempting. Making images is no riskier than making words. Indeed, there are two commandments against abusing words but only one against abusing images.

The common ground for all our words, images, and acts is the same mix of good and evil that is in us all. The devil can quote words of scripture as well as entice us with images of power, wealth, beauty, fame, or success.

I felt sadness for my pastor friend and many others of us Protestants who have seen images only as potential idols and demons and have thus missed so much by subduing the visual arts in favor of the verbal word. But the sadness came with the new understanding that despite the danger of images, the risks are no more than the risks of misused words. It also came with a sense of joy that we can let those with ears hear and let those with eyes see (Matthew 13:16). To believe that creation was meant to be lived in joy and grace is to see a new vision with unscaled eyes. I gradually decided that I would start balancing my words with images, my reading with sketching, and my hearing with seeing. Along with my daily journal I now carry a sketchbook.

Creativity

The power of images compared to words started to become clear to me during the Vietnam War. I remember a thin, nervous man who came to my office at the White Church. He was on a mission he did not like. An inactive member of the church, he sat down and got right to the point. The local American Legion Post sent him to question me about my "teaching young men to dodge the draft." I told him that I sought to inform them of their option of conscientious objection to the war in Vietnam, but that this terrible choice was up to each individual conscience. And a good decision required detailed knowledge of available options. My church denomination had long supported conscientious objection as an ethical alternative to being taken into the military and fighting in war. I felt it was my duty to so inform them, but the decision was theirs, not mine. He did not seem prepared for my response and eventually left, seeming puzzled.

My war protesting puzzled a number of my parishioners. I heard rumblings about my actions and worried that I could lose my job. But I saw my protests as a moral necessity and preached, taught, held teach-ins at the church, joined demonstrations, wrote letters to editors, lobbied my congressional representatives, withheld some of my taxes, and later even went to jail briefly to protest the Vietnam War. But the war dragged on year after year, gaining its own momentum. No one seemed to take responsibility for it. Every legislator I called on blamed someone else. I came to understand how evil worked on its own, sucking in draftees, noncombatants, and whole nations into a treacherous storm of death. It put soldiers in impossible spiritual, moral, and physical pain with no hero's welcome on their return— if they returned. How could we talk about such evil so we could resist it effectively? Words seemed to make no difference. I searched for a language that could carry the heavy weight of this urgent moral issue that few in my parish seemed to care about unless they or a relative was drafted.

A brief word study is needed here. As the war continued seemingly on its own, the word "juggernaut" was used to try to depict this self-propulsion in which no one seemed accountable. We in the church peace movement searched for appropriate words such as "idolatry" of the nation or flag. But "idol" had little efficacy, and it was too passive to grasp the active force that drove the war making. In the Bible, "idol" was largely replaced with "demon(s)" in the Christian Scriptures. "Idol" is never mentioned in the Gospels, but "demon(s)" take over (used sixty-two times) along with "Satan" (used twenty-two times) in the Christian Scriptures. They help name the self-willed force of evil. "Demons" and "Satan" are personifications of evil, which take on the human traits of a will, consciousness, and strategies of their own. However, such personification did not communicate. Except for those in very conservative churches, few people take demons or Satan seriously in their daily lives. Anthropomorphic demons and Satan suggest archaic notions of witchcraft and voodoo worship. Yet who would doubt the evil force of war? So what could we call such evil that has its own corporate power without scaring people off with personalized concepts of demons and Satan?

In an age dominated by a psychological worldview, words that were substituted for these biblical terms were "obsession," "possession," and "compulsion." We began to speak of U.S. leaders as "obsessed" with the fear of communism in Vietnam, "possessed" by the need to win a war, and caught in a "compulsive" mind-set that denied facts staring them in the face, such as the nationalist motivation of Vietnam finally to throw off the servitude of Western colonialism—a motivation ironically similar to our own in the U.S. revolution to overthrow our colonial rule by England. But psychological terms have limited historic weight. The frustrations with finding a language to speak of the war were further complicated by the daily news releases of Orwellian doublespeak by the military of "body counts" and "light at the end of the tunnel."

Where words failed, it took something else to communicate that the war was an evil that was out of control and had to be stopped. It took images. I believe it took the photographic images of the My Lai massacre in 1968 and of the nine-year-old Pham Thi Kim, the burned girl fleeing naked from her bombed village in 1972, to break through to enough people to form a critical mass of voting citizens to stop the war. The art of photography did what words failed to do to end the war. This is, of course, an unprovable opinion. But in the early 1970s the war began to wind down, and my church gradually tolerated my activism. The most convincing evidence of the power of imagery was what the military did in response to photojournalism. While military spokespersons issued gobbledygook by the buckets, the images of war were being broadcast all over the world. They eventually realized that new satellites could broadcast such images worldwide in seconds and the ugliness of war could not be hidden unless they controlled photojournalists' access to battle scenes. That is exactly what the military has done in all the wars since Vietnam.

Without consciousness of any of this hindsight I began sculpting images of Vietnam. In the late sixties I sculpted one piece that I called *War*. (See figure 2, *War*, page 37.) I had seen a magazine photo of a Vietnamese family huddling together while their village was destroyed by napalm and antipersonnel bombs from U.S. planes. I made a ceramic sculpture inspired by this image, which became the first one I showed publicly. I saw it as an attempt visually to break the evil possession of the war at least for myself. My word study led me to try to understand the power of visual "language," which in turn led me to try to make sense of "modern art." As powerful as photographic images are, drawing, painting, and sculpture in modern and postmodern art have defused their power for average people, becoming in some cases inaccessible and even elitist. There is a profound disconnect between modern and postmodern art and the general public.[1] Why?

Breaking idols or obsessions has been one of the purposes of the visual arts. Artistic imagery has both a destructive and a constructive purpose. But recently, the visual arts generally have been possessed with only one side of this dual purpose. That one side is the breaking of the old, the past, the idols of an age, real or imagined. The visual arts (sculpture, painting, photography) have, since around 1913, set out to destroy the old by ever-new imagery that provokes and disturbs, usually by destruction or extreme distortion of recognizable figures. Even to be considered art by many galleries, critics, and modern art museums is to be unique, new, original with the power (however momentary) to shock.

Picasso said, "Every act of creation is first of all an act of destruction."[2] Recent movements in art from abstract expressionism to pop and op, from performance art to destructivism and many others, broke new ground and in so doing not only broke old images of what was considered good art, but also made the very definition of art itself new, unique, and ever changing. All standards were rejected. Art was art if the artist said it was. With enough uniqueness, shock, and gallery connections, such an artist got shown and bought.[3]

This is not necessarily bad or wrong. Unique images that break the petrified and possessive forms (idols and demons) of the past are essential and are a traditional role of visual art. Picasso's *Guernica* is a profound and prophetic judgment on fascism. But breaking the old is only half the purpose of art. Creative artists break down the old images and destroy idols, but they also try to give form to chaos. In the formation of chaos is beauty, the other purpose of art. By making order out of life's apparent disarray, truth and beauty are revealed in the imagination. Both destruction and construction are indispensable aspects of creativity.

We need fresh images and words when old images and words fail to break through demonic entrapments such as war. But we also need a broad definition of visual art that affirms the constructive forming of chaos into beauty as well as the destructive uniqueness that breaks the old.

This understanding guided my development as an artist. I never felt the urge to abandon figurative imagery, though I appreciate many other works that do. One cannot hide in figurative art, for in incorrect form, especially anatomy, mistakes glare for all to see. Although good anatomy is a craft and only a means, "the artist who neglects it will never attain his end, which is the interpretation of feeling," according to Rodin. "Incorrect anatomy would raise a laugh when the artist wished to be touching. . . . An arm which is too short, a leg which is not straight, an inexact perspective, repels the spectator. In short, no sudden inspiration can replace the long toil which is indispensable to give the eye a true knowledge of form and of proportion and to render the hand obedient to the commands of feeling."[4]

I am especially moved by beautifully crafted human figures. In the late 1970s I spent three years modeling a sculpture. (See figure 3, *Second Birth,* page 38.) It began with the clay modeling of a live model in a class I took. But it was barely started when the class moved on to another model and another pose. I brought the unfinished piece home, though I had no work space for it or even a sculpture stand.

I jury-rigged a post from an old floor lamp into a stand, hung a light in the basement, and kept working on the clay model. Although I continually studied the anatomy of models in classes, I realized I had to learn anatomy from the bones out. Month after month I saw something was wrong in this piece and I did not know what it was, but I had no live model to compare and find my answer. So I bought and studied many books on anatomy. Yet I rarely found a picture that matched the particular posture of an arm or leg that I sought. I even constructed a skeleton and layers of muscles to grasp the shape of the human frame. I learned that it takes a lifetime to understand anatomy well. Every movement of any part of the body changes its image in an infinite variety of shapes.

I wanted to sculpt a human figure that *showed* rather than *told* about my feelings in those days. They were feelings of great struggle with my demons of the past but also the hope that a new self was emerging from the battle. In the final form of the sculpture, one hand and one foot grasp on to the known past; the other hand and foot accept the unknown future. The whole posture unfolds like a child in birth. I named it *Second Birth* because I believe our lives are a series of rebirths if we are blessed with the gift of letting go of the old demons and with the gift of forming new lives from the chaos. Constructing beauty or formed chaos must, I believe, be balanced with the destructive uniqueness that transcends the congealed images of the past. Such beauty is experienced as unexpected reprieve or grace. If it is not balanced with the destructively new, its beauty becomes a sentimental reworking of dying demons and obsessions of the past that worked once but no more. This is the problem of too much "church art." Likewise, the destructive uniqueness of the ever-new image must be balanced with the constructive forming of chaos into beauty. Such uniqueness is experienced with discomfort and challenge to move off old mental pictures. But if such destruction is not balanced with beauty of formed chaos, the wreckage is only that, wreckage that becomes cynical and despairing. This is the problem of too much "gallery art."

This balanced process of overcoming the demons and creating new forms of beauty is not only a useful definition of art; it is a redemptive way to live one's life, I believe. I cast *Second Birth* into bronze as a reminder.

Art and
Social Justice

After the Vietnam War ended in the 1970s, the United States shifted its counterinsurgency warfare to Central America. I shifted my sculpture to images of the victims of this Central American campaign. (See figure 4, *Witness;* figure 5, *The Wall: El Salvador;* figure 6, *The Fall;* figure 7, *Interrogation: Guatemala,* pages 40–47.) One evening I read an article about a Honduran woman who had been severely tortured by the Honduran security agents; she learned that they were trained by the U.S. Central Intelligence Agency (CIA).[1] In fact, she said a U.S. agent was present during her torture. She said she would have been killed like many others had her father not known people in important positions in the Honduran military. He was able to get her released eventually. Her name is Inez. Reading details of her torture was painful. Realizing that, as a U.S. citizen, I too was responsible for it felt worse. I went to my studio and worked most of the night sculpting a piece on her ordeal as I imagined it. (See figure 8, *Honduran Woman,* page 48.) Of course, it made no difference to anyone. Changing national policy takes long, hard political organizing over years to make the least bit of difference, as we learned during the Vietnam War. I needed to sculpt this piece as a personal response to this grievous information in addition to pursuing my political activities against the U.S. policy of teaching and supporting torture in Central America.

However, I struggled with the problem of using my art for political goals. Was I only doing propaganda? Many artists avoid politically charged issues for good reasons. Promoting a political cause, or especially a particular politician, risks artists' integrity and their standing among other artists. The logic goes: art has its own integrity, and when used for political ends (or religious or any other ends than its own; "art for art's sake," the slogan says), it becomes derivative at least and corrupted at most by narrow, passing political matters. In a word, it becomes propaganda, not art. One example of art as propaganda is the Soviet realism of the Stalin period. Another is the beautifying realism, to use Tillich's phrase, that the Nazis promoted over what they called "decadent art" of some of the greatest twentieth-century artists such as Käthe Kollwitz and Ernst Barlach. Both artists used their drawing and sculpture for the causes of peace, justice, humanity, the poor and oppressed, but were banned by the Nazis. However, no one doubts now the artistic greatness of their work.

Even art using themes of peace and justice may risk being labeled as propaganda by those with opposing views. It is often the judgment of history (and the winner's history at that) that is left to distinguish between art and propaganda. I searched for answers to this dilemma in art history. Three sculptors are generally considered the greatest in Western history: Phidias, Michelangelo, and Rodin. All had political involvements. In 438 B.C.E. in Greece, Phidias was arrested, tried, and convicted for using his sculpture as a "sacrilege" and was either exiled or died in jail, according to differing accounts. Michelangelo sided with the republican cause in Florence in the 1500s. He designed and directed the building of its defensive barricades until politics drove him into hiding to save his life from the Medici armies. Rodin, apparently against his will, was involved in the Dreyfus Affair through his much-condemned sculpture of Balzac in the 1890s. He also said his *Thinker* represented workers who were trying to organize to fight injustice in his time.[2]

Closer to our time and in our country is Ben Shahn, who was deeply involved in political action and is revered as one of our great artists. Shahn was a New Deal liberal and a Works Progress Administration (WPA) artist who engaged in poster art, lithographs, and paintings that promoted many causes for peace and justice, such as the opposition to the execution of Sacco and Vanzetti, and the Rosenbergs. He used his art for union organizing, antipoverty programs, antifascist causes, and antiwar, civil rights, United Nations, and environmental issues. He was threatened by the notorious House Un-American Activities Committee, but he did not back down. He took them on and fought with his art and his speech. He publicly said, "The world effect of the Un-American Activities Committee has been more than once to turn us into an international laughing stock, to lose us respect and friendship on every hand, to earn us the reputation of being a Philistine nation—which we are not."[3]

Shahn's haunting imagery of the depression and the many victims of poverty, injustice, discrimination, and war helped to depict an era in U.S. history that defined us as a people. Yet he did not hesitate to speak up and draw out his political views. How could he do art with integrity and political action at the same time? What was his secret? Early in the 1950s when the "Red scares" were beginning, Shahn spoke up for the morality of art and poetry:

> The time is past due for us to decide whether we are a moral people, or merely a comfortable people, whether we place our own convenience above the struggle of backward nations, whether we place the sanctity of enterprise above the debasement of our public. If it falls to the lot of artists and poets to ask these questions, then the more honorable their role. It is not the survival of art alone that is at issue, but the survival of the free individual and a civilized society.[4]

Shahn believed that the rise of abstract art in this period was influenced by the political repression of the political right wing. He said, "Abstract painting is, politically speaking, about the most non-committal statement that can be made in art. . . . Abstract art had left its political banners far behind, and for many years gone its way, disengaged."[5]

To be disengaged was not possible for Shahn. To fight the evils of his time was necessary for the artist as a human being. Shahn combined art and politics. He considered it an artist's duty to fight evil.

I gradually came to understand that an artist is one who attends with extreme sensitivity to the spirit of an age and presents its images with the greatest possible technical skill combined with uniqueness and beauty that form the chaos of that age. Like the serious person of faith, art must be engaged *in* the world, but not *of* the world; caring but critical of the human enterprise in that artist's time; engaged to suffer with the people, but also detached to observe the spiritual forces at work; challenging the idols and demons and offering visual images (visions) of beauty, grace, and goodness.

For me there were risks to choosing "political" subjects for my art because it may be easily dismissed as propaganda or ideology. But the moral loss of ignoring the cruel treatment of people and nature was an even greater risk. Too many German artists and Christians ignored Hitler's atrocities. And too many artists and Christians in the United States have ignored the atrocities we have committed against others, such as the native people of this land. I chose to be engaged.

This understanding has guided my art and inspired me to sculpt pieces not only of Central American peasants, who were mostly Indians, but also of other oppressed people, such as North American Indians. My full-time job for the last few years has given me the rare opportunity to learn firsthand about American Indians. My task has been to monitor federal legislation that affects Indians and to help them fight for their treaty rights, which are chronically ignored and abused by Congress. I have also met with Indians for three-day conferences in the northern plains states twice a year, often on reservations.

I learned on the reservations and in Washington, D.C., how our profound ignorance of Indians is the first level of our shameful treatment of them. I began to write a number of articles on these issues. I also wanted to sculpt images of American Indians for a long time, but I hesitated because I felt that only Indians had a right to name themselves and create their own images of themselves. Many whites have painted and sculpted caricatures of noble Indians, usually men on horseback. I did not want be a part of that because such caricatures obscure the truth of what we Europeans did to them.

When I was commissioned to make a sculpture for a chapel of the United Church of Christ office near Madison, Wisconsin, I changed my mind. I had been sculpting South American Indians for some time. Why not North American Indians if I could avoid some of the stereotypes? The conference minister, Frederick Trost, gave me the commission, with the only guideline that it was to show God's presence in the world. It would be called *Emmanuel*, meaning "God with us." It occurred to me that if I had only a single image of God's presence in the land we named Wisconsin, I should choose to represent a people who had been there hundreds of years, the Hocak (Winnebago). Even though the U.S. Army had tried to push them beyond the Mississippi, they returned to Wisconsin. I chose to sculpt a Hocak woman supporting a young man and also holding her hand out in a gesture that could be either for offering bread or for begging. (See figure 9, *Emmanuel*, page 51.) Their arms are intertwined in common support. Her countenance expresses simple dignity in spite of her impoverished condition. I chose a woman because women are underrepresented. I believe God is present in the world, especially as people care for each other and especially in the "least of these" (Matthew 25:31–46). By all accounts American Indians are the "the least" among us as the most-deprived people in the United States. And except for demeaning caricatures as sports and commercial mascots, they are the most forgotten. I wanted to represent the reality of their poverty, illness, and dignity.

I made many other sculptures of "the least of these" people who were oppressed and tortured in Cambodia, Sri Lanka, South Africa, China, the United States, and elsewhere. But I see the human struggle to be spiritual as well as political. I have done many pieces on personal and spiritual struggles: despair, loneliness, liberation, joy, dreaming, and other internal human cares. (See figure 10, *Despair*; figure 11, *Down*; figure 12, *Adah*; figure 13, *Dreamer*; figure 14, *Harpist*; figure 15, *Hearing Angels*; figure 16, *Holy Communion*; pages 52–62.)

I spent months—sometimes years—making each sculpture. In each I searched for the depth and meaning of feeling on personal, social, and political levels. If we start with raw human experiences first before we impose on them words, labels, images, much less caricatures and stereotypes, we can begin to see our common humanity beneath the surface. I believe that to grasp this level of the common human spirit, we must believe that there is more than the powerful force of evil let loose in the world. If we believe evil does exist that can act through corporate agents beyond the power of individual human choice, then it is not a great stretch to believe that there also can be some glimmers of corporate goodness that are loose in the world. Such a belief in goodness allows us to see with unscaled eyes and to imagine a world of personal joy and social, and even political, justice. This belief allows us to see the good news, the visual gospel, even in the political world.

Sculpture and Poetry

I found rather late in my life that my love for others and my feeling of being loved by them increased to the degree that we acknowledged the complexity and mystery of each other's being. This realization came powerfully to me the first time I was asked to present my art to a conference of Christian social activists near Portland, Oregon. For the first time I would reveal some of my most private struggles through slides of my sculpture. I had no idea how they would be received or indeed whether I would expose myself as only a dilettante with a hobby who would embarrass himself and an audience of fifty or so people. I had a terrible struggle over what to show and to say. My sculpture comes from the deepest part of my being, and I do not understand what it all means.

But a wonderful thing happened as I set up my slide projector. One of the activists, a pastor in Brooklyn and a gifted musician, Bob Lepley, volunteered to play the piano during my slide show using a part of a new composition he had written on a Rainer Maria Rilke poem. The poem was "My life is not this steeply sloping hour in which you see me hurrying."[1] The poem continues to explain how truly complex and finally unknowable one individual person really is. As I began to reveal myself in my art, I too wanted to declare, "My life is not this steeply sloping hour in which you see me hurrying." My artistic self was a completely new part of me, strange to myself and unknown to these people who knew me before this only as a writer–activist–minister.

The poem expressed well my anxiety over being typecast as one thing (an amateur artist) when inside me there are three or four selves fighting like children for attention. I got through the session well enough, went home, and found and studied many of Rilke's poems. Since that time I have found that poetry often grasps what Rilke says about who he is not and expresses the real complexity of people and things, which is what I try to communicate in my sculpture. This poetry spoke deeply to me in contrast to our media-dominated culture. Instead of expressing the complexity of who people really are and of the events of the news, popular culture and the media pander to our weakness to simplify them. Multifaceted people are given the nondescript labels of "motorist," "housewife," "mom of four," and "drifter" in the news. Such oversimplification can easily lead to stereotyping and then to enemy objectification, which then falsely justifies hate and violence. By contrast, art and poetry at their best reveal the complexity of reality as we experience it, leaving room to honor and respect other beings who are complex beyond measure.

The paradox of love is that we know others (only in part), but we "unknow" others (in their complexity) at the same time. To know another intimately is not enough. One must "unknow" another to truly love him or her, that is, stand in awe of the mystery of another's being. I feel loved when another takes the time to learn some of who I am, yet also allows for much, much more before he or she tries to name who I am. I also realize how important it is to learn of another's life and cares but at the same time to recognize that I can see and know only a tiny part of who the other is. Respecting the unknown in others is especially critical among groups of people. The opposite is prejudice and fear that lead to war between such groups.

The apostle Paul said that we know and are fully known only beyond this life (1 Corinthians 13:12). To seek to express the rich (unknowable) complexity of oneself—and to seek that in others, yet never presuming to know more than one sees through a glass darkly—is to me the great task of art, especially poetry and visual art.

The most helpful book I have found on the creative process goes by the simple name *Creativity*. Otherwise this four-hundred-page book is not simple. It was written by Mihaly Csikszentmihalyi, professor of psychology at the University of Chicago. He studied ninety-one extremely creative people: Nobel laureates, artists, scientists, and standouts in many fields. He experienced difficulty when he tried to isolate the dominant traits to explain their creativity.

> Are there then no traits that distinguish creative people? If I had to express in one word what makes their personalities different from others, it would be *complexity*. By this I mean that they show tendencies of thought and action that in most people are segregated. They contain contradictory extremes—instead of being an "individual," each of them is a "multitude." Like the color white that includes all the hues in the spectrum, they tend to bring together the entire range of human possibilities within themselves.[2]

Certainly, complexity and diversity are not essential only in nature (biodiversity is key to life on earth). Respect for them is essential to human relations, and it is the key to artistic creativity. I am sure of this in sculpture and poetry and in sculptors and poets.

This connection that I discovered between sculpture and poetry began to bridge a vast gap in my psyche between the spoken and written word and visual images. Both poetry and sculpture seek to express the inexpressible, to honor the mystery, and to respect the complexity of being. This connection was happily locked in place for me when I met the poet Maren Tirabassi.

About a year after the Oregon conference, I had the opportunity to speak at a similar conference on art and social action in New York. Bob Lepley was the musician again, Maren was the poet, and I was the visual artist. I did not know her before this, but when I heard her read some of her work, I was very impressed and asked for copies of some of her poems so I could study them. She then asked me if she might write poems on my sculpture. I was delighted to say yes.

She wrote poems from photos of my sculpture that I sent her. I was amazed at her keen perception and fresh, nuanced phrasing. She grasped not only subtle aspects of the sculpture that I consciously intended, but also new perspectives that I recognized but did not consciously name. Her poetry challenged and encouraged me to learn and grow in very helpful ways. We began making a series of presentations of our work through sculpture slides and poetry on the sculpture at theological seminaries. After a while it occurred to us to reverse the process of Maren writing poems on my sculpture. I would sculpt from her poetry. So I made sculptures from her poems, such as "Holy Communion," "A Small Remembering," and "Adah's Song." (See figure 16, *Holy Communion*; figure 30, *Nun*; figure 12, *Adah*; pages 62, 89, 54.) Later we took a common theme, landmines, and wrote and sculpted pieces independently of each other's creative process. At the opening of my sculpture exhibit at Wesley Theological Seminary, we revealed our creations to each other and to an audience for the first time. I was shocked to see the commonality in our thinking. What I tried to say visually, she tried to picture verbally. We even included a soccer ball that the boy will never be able to play with because of the destruction of his leg by a landmine.

In many ways Maren and I hardly know each other. We have met face-to-face maybe six or seven times at public events, and the rest of our acquaintance has been through correspondence in which I comment on her poems and she writes poetry on my sculpture that is most fitting and insightful. For example, in the first poem she wrote on my sculpture "Hearing Angels," she described the waking body of a woman in vivid detail, then suggested the woman might be Joan of Arc or Mary of Nazareth who is hearing angels. (See figure 15, *Hearing Angels*, page 60.) I had not consciously thought of Joan or Mary or anyone else hearing angels while I was creating the work. Yet the words are a perfect fit for a deep motive I felt as I sculpted the piece; I tried to model a woman with dignity and alertness who is rising from one unknown to reach out for another mystery that is calling her.

The first sculpture I did from one of Maren's poems was *Holy Communion*. When I received the poem in the mail, I tacked it on an easel in my studio and read it many times until an image appeared to me. The image was a painting by Goya, *The Dream of Reason Brings Forth Monsters*. Even though the theme and body position were different, for me the image of a person leaning on a table fit the ending lines of the poem:

> *I took my bag-supper*
> *into the nighttime sanctuary,*
> *put the sandwich on the*
> *communion table,*
> *muttered a few words they teach*
> *pastors to say,*
> *and stood there in the dark*
> *to cry on the bread.*

I made an image of Maren leaning on the communion table holding the bread— bread that is the body of Christ present here also in the broken body of Cathy whom she had just lifted into her bed of death, a pietà. As I have read this poem and shown the sculpture to others, the identification with the experience of ministering to dying people is strong, and tears are frequent. I think many of us know the pain well. Hearing the poem also leads the hearer to feel she or he knows something very deep and personal about the author of the poem. Reading all of these poems that arise out of a profound search of the deepest insights, I feel I know many of the poet's secrets. I am sure that a careful viewing of my sculpture tells more of my secrets than I can ever reveal otherwise. Yet strangely, though these creations of our works reveal so much, they touch only the edge of our complexity. For me, at each deeper level of my being that I reach through artistic struggle, I see even more receding like the horizon. In the creative process I constantly discover new things about myself and about new images that emerge in the sculptures. In a sense the creative act takes charge of me.

I now appreciate why artists speak of muses guiding them beyond their control. Muses are angels without halos in that muses easily become demons. The creative process is full of surprises, mystery, and complexity. I never know what a sculpture will look like, even though I begin each with a clear image of what I want. Every piece reveals to me new things I had never thought of consciously. When Maren then writes about the piece, I learn much more that I had not known about myself, about her, and about the endless complexity of things.

Though I have come to know Maren very well through our correspondence and the exchanges of our art (we are both ordained ministers in the same denomination and share much in our theology and commitments to peace and justice issues), I am frequently startled to learn how much I do not know about her and how often I misunderstand things she says. We know each other, yet only through a glass darkly. We disagree frequently but stick to the task. That task is to show and to say in sculptural and poetic imagery that we can live blessed and joyous lives amid the vast chaos and unknowing. Indeed, the blessing and joy require us to honor the complexity and unknown aspects of creation. I believe this is an important calling.

We have dealt with much of the world's chaos in the subjects of our poetry and sculpture. I believe if we ignore this chaos in our world, we deny reality and are dishonest. But it is also wrong to ignore the persistence of goodness, joy, and hope, in spite of chaos. My purpose in my art is to discover that thread of goodness within this world's sorrows. The sculpture *Joy* and poem "Ode to Joy" attempt to express this explicitly. (See figure 38, *Joy*, page 105.) The woman bends "up into some wonderful presence / that I cannot see" and finds the "unexpected happiness of a child."

The narrative of this book began with a search for how we can find and keep the joy of unexpected reprieves, such as feeling "alive after illness." The clues to joy are all about us, of course, but we hide them and hide from them. For the clues to this joy are in the simplest things: the dirt, rock, and sunshine that in the gift of joy become "most profound," "the most unbelievably intense / and swiftly precious."

The answer to finding and keeping joy is both too simple and too complex. We have only to stop and look at the beauty of God's creation in the simplest stone or bit of soil. Yet we also must honor and dignify the dirt, clay, and mud by respecting their true complexity. The simple clay of sculpture is infinitely complex in its molecular structure before and after its vitrification in the kiln firing. As for the spiritual and moral complexity of standing sculptures, deciphering their meanings could fill a library. Examples are the monuments to Stalin and Lenin before and after the fall of the Soviet Union or Michelangelo's *Pietà* in Rome before and after it was vandalized. The paradox is that joy is found in the simplicity of all life, which is itself infinitely complex. When we join sculpture and poetry, the paradox increases so that we may stand awed by the simple beauty of the gifts of life's rich universe of multiversities. The beauty of this paradox is the good news I seek in the visual gospel.

Visual Arts in the Church and Community

I will conclude this narrative with practical suggestions for encouraging the visual arts and poetry in the church and community. It is a special blessing that I can do so from Wesley Theological Seminary, where I am currently artist-in-residence. About fifteen years ago Wesley established a Center for the Arts and Religion. Here the arts are taken seriously as part of theological education. Successful artists are invited to be artists-in-residence and are given studio space to create their works in the midst of the school. Such works are on display throughout the seminary. A formal art gallery keeps a regular schedule of exhibitions. Art courses are part of the required curriculum. The founder and director of the center is Catherine Kapikian, a nationally known artist with degrees in both art and theology.

After I had a solo exhibit at Wesley two years ago, Catherine invited me to return. I am spending three semesters (one and a half years) as artist-in-residence. I have time to finish this book, to interact with other artists-in-residence, students, and faculty, and to release a great energy flow into creating more and better sculptures than I thought possible. Finally, after thirty years of focusing my time on my regular job, with art squeezed in to what time I had left over, I can now direct more attention to art in a supportive environment. Instead of sculpting alone at night, I can do so in the day and night with other artists.

This has been a blessing to me personally, and it has suggested a number of ideas for the church that takes visual arts seriously. I believe that a large percentage of people are visually oriented like I am and are eager for visual communication and poetic expression. It is clear now that there is no reason whatsoever, biblically or theologically, for the church to continue the rejection of visual imagery. There remains, however, the job of showing *how* the church can encourage and employ the visual arts.

First, it is valuable to recognize that artistic designs are all around us. Even the pure white church sanctuary is a deliberate artistic design. Sculpture can be defined as three-dimensional designs in space that express the values of a person or community. Sculpture, so defined, is found in the church architecture, stained glass, furniture, altar, baptismal fonts, pulpits, candle holders, and even flower arrangements. All of these are artistic works that someone designed, regardless of their quality. Even cheap plastic communion cups were designed by someone, and our use of them expresses our values. There are no neutral spaces. We may be oblivious to these artistic designs, but where there is space in a building, the artistic designs are there for good or otherwise.

One of the artists with whom I was able to exchange ideas was Douglas Purnell, a painter-theologian on sabbatical from United Theological Seminary in Australia. I enjoyed reading and commenting on a book he was writing on art and theology. In it he says,

> Too often in our churches we seem satisfied with inadequate architecture, poorly designed space, poor art, poorly designed and constructed banners, sloppy music, amateur dramatics. If we have a visual in our churches we will have words dominate it as though we fear the rising of the spirit in response to something of sheer beauty, a rising that takes the soul beyond where mere words can go. Our fear of the imagination seems to run over into a fear of symbols, particularly eucharistic symbols where inadequate amounts of bread cut into the tiniest squares and over sweet grape juice dished out in the tiniest glasses is meant to represent something substantial and nourishing about God. When we have professional art or artists, we in the church seem embarrassed to use, acknowledge and remunerate them appropriately. (It would be more readily accepted in a church council that we pay someone to mow the lawn than that we pay an artist to decorate, dance or make music in our worship space.) How might it be received at the Centre for Ministry if we organised volunteers to hop on the tractor lawn-mower and used the money saved to employ a resident artist whose brief was to create works of art that might be used in the chapel?[1]

An obvious model for bringing visual arts and poetry into the church is the way in which we appreciate and use music in our churches. Music has always been welcomed in Protestant churches. The founders of Protestantism such as Martin Luther and Charles Wesley were often musicians as well as preachers and theologians. The combination of poetry and music in hymns is another powerful merging of two art forms as we propose in this book on poetry and sculpture.

What if a church hired a professional visual artist or poet as we hire professional organists and choir directors who bring and teach disciplined music for each worship service? A full- or part-time visual artist-poet could encourage the congregation's awareness of the church's values as they are already expressed visually in the church's structure, furniture, and worship space. The artist-poet could teach children, young people, and adults to express their faith in visual forms just as well as the choir director guides their disciplined musical expression.

A room or hallway could be set aside for art exhibits. Artists are usually so eager to show their art publicly, they will do most of the work for a display. Visual arts have to be seen publicly. The church is a public place where the celebration of creativity easily draws out talent and focuses artistic productivity. I recall years ago spending boundless energy on creating new sculptures when I was invited to have a meager part in a small church art exhibit.

A monthly exhibit of artworks with an opening, refreshments, and discussion with artists is an ideal way to support visual arts. Poetry readings also bring out some of the best spiritual concerns rarely expressed otherwise. I announced a poetry reading in church one Sunday, and twenty people showed up—with their poetry. These discussions provide an opportunity to raise theological questions dealing with preverbal, preconceptual experience (faith precedes words, images, and thoughts) that is expressed visually and poetically. A first and inexpensive step toward hiring a visual artist-poet may be to designate an artist or poet with the honorary title of artist- or poet-in-residence at the church with specific duties for a season.

My church pastor and then the Board of Deacons at Christ Congregation in Princeton, New Jersey, asked me to design and make candleholders for the altar. (See figure 39, *Candle Holders*, page 106.) For eight months I thought about this project and carried the image in my mind of worshiping in the sanctuary with my sculpture on the altar in full view of God and the congregation. It was an awesome challenge. Yet since no neutral space exists, my candleholders would replace two tacky plastic dishes that had been there with no real religious meaning.

I decided to render two sets of hands (one, a pair of rough, struggling hands; the other, soft, graceful hands), both holding forth candles of sacred light and reaching up for that light. Church members repeatedly express their appreciation for the way that these visual sermons speak to their spiritual concerns. Knowing that a part of my creativity sits on the altar of my church is an honor and a strong motivation for greater participation in the life of the church. This could be the experience of artists in your congregation.

Flower arranging is a very high art form, especially in Japan. It should be encouraged and refined with expert coaching and disciplined instruction of both the arrangers and the congregation, who can always meditate on the flowers ("Consider the lilies of the field . . .") whatever the verbal messages may be communicating during the service of worship. My colleague Douglas Purnell suggests that occasionally, we place paintings on the altar instead of flowers. He did that many times in his home church in Australia and at the Wesley Seminary Chapel when we co-led a communion service there. His abstract expressionist triptych hung above the altar, calling forth a visual naming of the sacred that is beyond words. In place of an all-verbal sermon, he drew an image of Jesus at the table on a large sheet of paper. I displayed the sculpture *Holy Communion* and read Maren's poem of that name. Afterward a student came to the studio and told us we did one thing wrong. I braced for her critique. She said we should have provided Kleenex.

One does not need to have original art in the worship service to "preach" visual sermons like this. I have used slides and duplicated copies of paintings and sculpture. Slide projection allows one to give high focus to different aspects of a work of art. Prints or slides of biblical stories by Rembrandt, Dürer, Michelangelo, and many others are excellent visual sermons and can be bought or borrowed from museums. The photos of sculpture with the matching poems in this book can be used in place of a fifteen- to twenty-minute sermon.

We immediately adapt to the visual "look" of spaces in our churches. Newcomers quickly pick up on what we deem significant from the visual signs on our walls, our decorations, architecture, and furniture. Try to imagine coming to your church and seeing it for the first time. Are the spaces tacky with mundane announcements or rich in Christian symbols? Are they empty of meaning or full of witness to our faith? Are they neglected and left collecting dust or shiny with proud visuals of our traditions? What newcomers first see can mean falling in love at first sight or more church shopping.

Confirmation, new member, adult education, and Bible study classes and prayer group meetings are ideal opportunities to use visual arts and poetry. One can also plan trips to artists' studios and art museums and invite artists and poets to speak about and to show/read their artwork. The faithful visual witnesses of our artists are of equal merit to the written and verbal witnesses of saints and theologians. Remember that many of us are visually oriented, and a sculpture or painting of the crucifixion, for example, is more powerful than a verbal or written description of it. However, when the words of poetry and images come together, the Spirit is set loose. I believe Michelangelo was the greatest sculptor. Few know he was also a published poet. But first and last he was a devout Christian. Late in his life he said in a poem that it was not painting and sculpture that calmed his soul, but only Christ whose open arms on the cross take us in.[2]

Artists who seek to praise God with visual expressions along with musical, verbal, and written forms want to give their gifts to the church. If their visual content frightens people who worry about its orthodoxy, such fear is groundless, for the creative process itself is in part a sacred experience. The visual proclamation is, with all our human frailties, as true a witness as any other form of receiving and sharing the unexpected reprieve of grace.

sculptures

and poems

1. Landmines. *Ceramic. Artist's collection.*

Landmines

Landmines
aren't a part of anyone's story.
They are not aimed,
like a bullet or a knife.
They are not intended
for this child's left leg,
or the right half
of that young woman's face.
They are the
indiscriminate
story-breakers—
they are the waiting-death
under the feet
of all our stories.

They reach up from the ground
and take all the names away.
They leave the world
anonymous,
and more afraid of peace
than war.

They are the planted screaming
under all our jaws
and whispers;
they are the shit of war
when war is gone.

They are the patient waiters
which invite us
to imagine we are fully alive,
alive with tenderness and plans,
alive with possibilities
for joy and sadness,
for worries, achievements,
and complications,
for writing letters and playing soccer,
for dreaming and praying,
dozing and fighting,
marrying and grieving and
hoping,
for thinking about sex,
and making love,
or Sunday dinner,
or a mistake—
they invite us to imagine
we are fully alive
and matter to God
just before
we step on hell.

War

By war we are bound together
and we are torn apart.

We walk through the gallery of the
sculpture of war
past Achilles and Hector—
naked chest, shield, spear, naked heel,
Amazons, too, with bows taut,

past armored and equestrian knights—
the chivalry of lance and mace,
the crusader rampant
and in effigy,

past the generals and the privates
of Valley Forge and Waterloo,
the desperate of the Alamo,
and the fallen ones of Gettysburg,

past Teddy Roosevelt,
forever rough, forever gallant,
charging up the hill,

past images of new war—
orange poppy fields
and broken Coventry Cathedral,
soldiers, frozen in history,
raising a flag on an atoll,
photographs of Auschwitz and
of a Vietnamese girl napalm-naked,

past women buddies,
remembered in bronze,
and the black wall of memory,
mirror, and names.

Now the artist comes to our day,
and here is war—only this,
the one truth
that the sculpture can tell
of then and now and always—
of family, any family, all the families,
desperately clinging to one another—
hugging in the moment
before they become body parts.
Trojan Horse, Guernica,
statue of the needlessness of death.

2. War. Ceramic. Courtesy of Jerry Douglas Leggett and Drenda Tigner.

3. Second Birth. *Bronze, second edition.*
Artist's collection.

Second Birth

To trust the wind
and the kindness of the womb,

to be naked again,
to be named,
to be wet
    and held
and learn again to walk and speak,

to give up security
for the translucent riskiness
    of grace—
this is second birth.

Nicodemus . . .
looks in the lonely for the
riddle of existence.

Nicodemus . . .
trusts the Spirit,
and the teacher he finds
    in the night
and begins to be born.

Witness	El Testigo
Somewhere between the witness	En alguna parte entre el testigo
which is eye-witness	que es testigo visual
and the witness which	y el testigo que
is word-witness	es el testigo que habla
she hovers—eyes glance away,	ella vacila—ojos de mirada ausente,
lids fallen,	parpados caídos,
fingers to mouth	dedos en la boca
to press it mute,	para presionarlos mudos,
crouched or kneeling	encogida o arrodillada
to be small,	para verse más pequeña,
as if	como si
the sculptor knew	el escultor supiese
she wanted to hide	que ella quiere esconderse
and set her there in	y quedarse allí
cruel carven stone,	carvada el la cruda piedra,
exposed to the great pain, the	expuesta al gran dolor, a la
emergency	emergencia
of her witness.	de ser testigo.
And all we know	y todo lo que sabemos
is that	es que
she must see and	ella debe ver y
she must speak,	ella debe hablar,
she has seen and	ella ha visto y ella hablará,
she will speak,	y por su testimonio
and by her testimony	nosotros nos volveremos
we too become	miedo y piedra
fear and stone	y jurado.
and	
jury.	

4. Witness. Bronze.
Courtesy of Rev. Charlotte H. Still.

The Wall: El Salvador

The woman weeps in the wall,
her figure impressed
on square stones.
She presses cloth against
her weeping eyes,
face contorted with grief—
and there is no sound.

She will not tell who or how many.

A son or daughters, a mother,
a husband, sister,
village bodies or pieces
of bodies in a mass grave,
a priest, neighbors,
a grandchild,
and perhaps also rape,
or a burned house,
fields of corn, soul.

On the other side of the cloth
burned into it by her tears
are features of crucifixion,
a fabric stigmata from
a miracle or hell.

5. The Wall: El Salvador. *Ceramic relief.*
Artist's collection. Inspired by photo by Adam Kufeld
in El Salvador *(New York: Norton, 1990), 177.*

We, useless and hard,
like square gravestones
or long prayers,
pray—
for such a cloth,
may there be a shrine,
for such a woman,
some hope of relief. . . .
We ask, looking above her,

Is the wall broken, or are those stairs?

La Pared: El Salvador

La mujer llora
en la pared,
su figura está impresa
en las piedras cuadradas.
Ella aprieta su paño
contra sus
ojos llorosos,
su cara se contorna
con el dolor y no
hace ningún ruido.

Ella no dirá quien o cuantos.

Un hijo o hijas,
una madre,
un esposo, hermana,
cuerpos de una aldea o pedazos
de cuerpos amontonados
en una tumba,
un sacerdote, vecinos,
un nieto,
y quizás también violación
o una casa quemada,
campos de maíz, alma.

En el otro lado del paño
quemado por las lágrimas
están los rasgos de la crucifixión,
material de stigma de
un milagro o de un infierno.

Nosotros, inútiles y duros
como piedras cuadradas
o como largas oraciones,
ora—
por semejante paño,
quizás haya un resplandor,
para semejante mujer,
alguna esperanza de alivio …
Nos preguntamos, mirándola por encima,

Está la pared rota, o son esas las escaleras?

6. The Fall. *Bonded bronze. Artist's collection.*

The Fall

I, who am strong,
am bound.
I, who should flex
my muscles,
am bruised.
I, whose nostrils flare
like a stallion's,
whose eyes are sunk deep
with pride
and knowing;
whose mouth is full
with a passion of words,
but whose elbows are
lashed to my side,
am a man
without power.

Yet there is a rage
that twists
me into standing,
like a wick is twisted,
or a soul,
and the rage is my flame
and my fall.

La Caída

Yo, que soy fuerte,
estoy limitado.
Yo, quien debo flexionar
mis músculos,
estoy amoratado.
Yo, quien tiene la nariz enrojecida
como un caballo,
cuyos ojos están profundamente undidos
con orgullo
y conocimiento;
cuya boca está llena
de palabras pasionadas,
pero cuyos codos están
amarrados a un lado,
soy un hombre
sin poder.

Aún así hay en mi una furia
que me tuerse
para tratar de enderezarme,
como un pábilo se tuerse,
o un alma,
y la furia es mi llama
y mi caída.

Everything	Todo
Everything	**Todo**
Interrogation in Guatemala,	El Interrogatorio en Guatemala,
with blindfolds, stakes,	con vendas, apuestas, esposados,
handcuffs,	lazados, puyados,
bonds, goads,	cigarillos, violación,
cigarettes, rape, lights.	luces.
Interrogation has	El Interrogatorio no
nothing	tiene nada que ver
to do with questions,	con las preguntas,
everything	tiene que ver
to do with power.	con el poder.
Interrogation has	El Interrogatorio no
nothing	tiene nada que ver
to do with questions,	con las preguntas,
everything	tiene que ver
to do with pain.	con el dolor.
Interrogation in Guatemala,	El Interrogatorio en Guatemala,
courage, silence,	corage, silencio,
long waiting,	larga espera,
for the son,	por el hijo,
of a woman who weaves.	de una mujer que teje.
Interrogation has	El interrogatorio no
nothing	tiene nada que ver
to do with questions,	con las preguntas,
everything	tiene que ver
to do with hope.	con la esperanza.

7. Interrogation: Guatemala. *Ceramic. Courtesy of Jerry Douglas Leggett and Drenda Tigner.*

Returned to the Earth

The sculptor called it *Honduran Woman*
after an article
in the *Baltimore Sun,*
about a woman who had been tortured
by Honduran security forces
trained by the CIA
because she was suspected
of being a Marxist,
connected somehow
to a guerrilla group.

She was celled in solitary confinement
without her clothes
and the tender, private places
of her flesh received electric shock
and cigarette burns—
the usual—but just before her
disappearance could be completed,
her father made contact
with a childhood friend
well-placed in the military
and she was released
without explanation.

After that the Honduran woman
was very quiet.

Her friends said she changed
and was hard to visit,
and when she spoke,
her eyes would look away.
She even tried to live in the
    United States for a while,
but it didn't work out.

For a long time only as a photograph
was this sculpture of a woman,
naked on her knees
with her faced turned up
expecting her death.
The original was not fired
because the clay was wet and dry
too many times.
Unfinished, it crumbled,
and returned to the earth.

Haunted by the woman in his dreams
the sculptor made her again.

Alive, not forgotten, Inez.

8. Honduran Woman. *Ceramic. Artist's collection.*

Volver Al Polvo de la Tierra

El escultor la llama *La Mujer Hondureña*
después del artículo en la revista
Baltimore Sun,
sobre una mujer que fue torturada
por las fuerzas de seguridad Hondureñas
entrenados por la CIA
porque ella era sospechosa
de ser marxista,
conectada de alguna manera
a un grupo guerrillero.

Ella fue encerrada en una celda solitaria
desnuda
y en las delicadas partes privadas
de su cuerpo recibió choques eléctricos
y quemaduras de cigarrillos—
lo usual—pero antes de que
desapareciera por completo,
su padre contacto
a un amigo de la infancia
de buena reputacion militar
y a ella la soltaron
sin explicación alguna.

Después de esto la mujer hondureña
estaba muy callada.

Sus amigos decian que ella había cambiado
y que era díficil visitarla,
y, cuando hablaba,
sus ojos miraban desviados.
Ella aún trato de vivir
en los Estados Unidos por un tiempo,
pero no sirvió de nada.

Por mucho tiempo como una fotografía
era ésta escultura de mujer,
desnuda de rodillas
con su cara volteada
esperando la muerte.
La original no fue quemada
porque el barro se había mojado y secado
muchas veces.
Sin terminar, se desmenuzó,
y volvió al polvo de la tierra.

Perseguido por la mujer en sus sueños
el escultor la hizo nuevamente.

Viva, la no olvidada, Inez.

Prayer

The two bodies in the prayer
are kneeling.

He leans against her
in the hollow of shelter
between shoulder and breast.
He holds the fabric of her shirt
for balance
and for comfort.
He is smaller, younger,
more afraid than she.

She holds him, grasps his ribs
a gentle pressure,
but in her spine, the stance
of her quiet,
and in her looking ahead
for both of them,
she tells him in a hundred
silent sentences
that he will not fall.

The cane is there,
and the cup in fragile fingers
for begging, is there,
because life has given her
a begging cup.

She does not ask it away.

Many people come
to the chapel of prayer
and find them—
the woman with eyes like Jesus
and the young man
who needs her strength.

The people pray their own stories,
and their own need for
balance and comfort,
for remembering
what it is to look forward,
and what it is to look down
at their own crutches
and cups,
and then they pray
for the people who have
held arms around them,
and the people
they have embraced.

9. Emmanuel. *Ceramic. Courtesy of
Wisconsin Conference, United Church
of Christ, Rev. Frederick Trost,
Conference Minister.*

10. Despair. *Ceramic. Artist's collection.*

I am a statue, despair

I bow down my head
and it is almost a gesture in
the topography of emptiness.
I see my body—
the dish where I
have been
bread,
the dirt of my breast where

once bloomed
flowers.
I can no longer run to the
place beyond tears—
I am a statue, despair,
a graven thing,
without
epitaph.

Down

Not Rodin—not thinker.

Not Michelangelo—not David,
no sling, no conquest,
no youth.

Not the statues of city plazas.

Of course, neither is it Van Gogh
nor Toulouse-Lautrec
because there is no color,
not Rilke, Kafka, Sexton,
nor Virginia Woolf
because there are no words.

But, after all, it is more like these
than the sculptors of Hero.

Here is the art of Down—
with legs folded,
and bowed face-cheek

passively drooping
on fist, on elbow,
on knee,
while bowed face-eyes
look in-down.

It has become a self-portrait
of everyone
who can remember
some too-long
yesterday,
and a self-portrait of everyone
who will wake up
some damn-lonely tomorrow.

11. Down. *Ceramic. Artist's collection.*

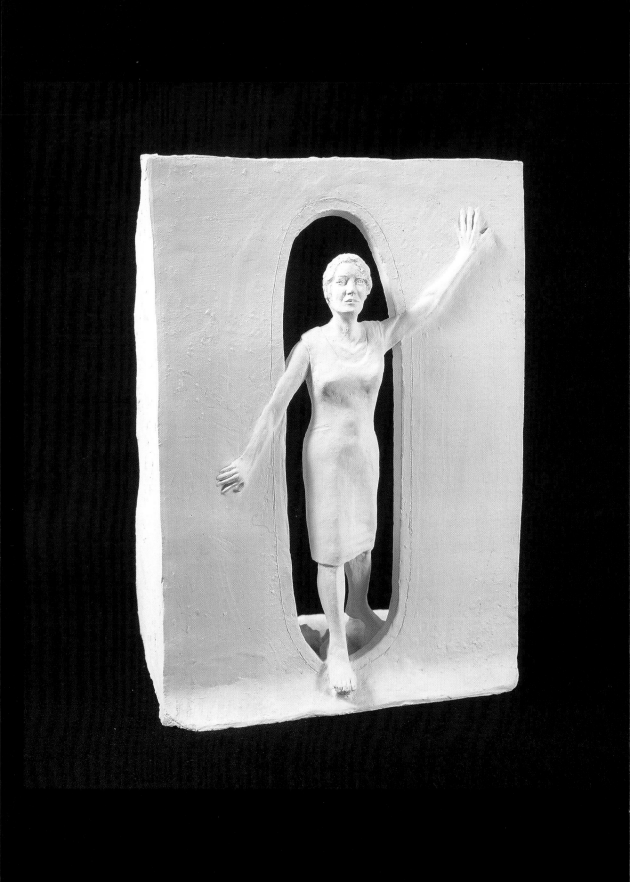

Adah's Song

The beauty burns
against the blue of morning sky
and I
in salt of weeping
look back
at the bright catastrophe
of all that meant too much
and my tears dry.

Remember me, Aunt Sarah.
Remember me,
daughters with your bellies
big with nations.
Remember me—
not as somebody's wife,
not as immobile,
but remember me
as the woman who
didn't need to run
anymore.

I have found my own place
in the wilderness,
and where I am
is holy.
I watch the sky blaze
an orange and pink and
golden past;
I lift my face to the soft rain

of falling ash;
I pray softly
and listen
to the whisper of
clean fire.

Reach out and touch me,
the smooth, the white of me;
lick the sea-dried taste
of my escape;
do not be afraid.
Take comfort
in me—
because
I am the woman who
stands still.

12. Adah. *Ceramic. Artist's collection.*

The Dreamer

The girl on the rock in the
wilderness of imagination
is dreaming—
she is dreaming of justice
and a chance for peace
for all the world's children.

13. Dreamer. *Ceramic. Artist's collection.*

The girl on the rock in the
wilderness of imagination
with her hair drawn back
and her eyes wide open
is dreaming—
she is dreaming of a lover
who will walk by her side
in the cool dawn and
still be there at nightfall.

The girl on the rock in the
wilderness of imagination
with her hair drawn back
and her eyes wide open and
her young breasts not-nursed
and her hands loose
is dreaming—
she is dreaming of her mother
and sorrow, and angels
and Jesus and the place that
is heaven and death . . .

she is dreaming of one candle flame,
and one starfish in a tidal pool,
a pine bough with snow
and a small grey bird.

The girl on the rock in the
wilderness of imagination
with her hair drawn back
and her eyes wide open and
her young breasts not-nursed
and her hands loose,
who is not sure she has
ever been awake,
is dreaming—

she is dreaming of life.

The Harpist

Where does the music come from?

The still lips,
the closed eyes
and soft face, slightly inclined,
leaning against the warm
grain of wood . . . or

the two embracing arms,
tense hands plucking
and fingers in fierce caress?

Where does the music come from?

A sail of bentwood,
the fragile vibrating air
between the bright, taut filament
of rippling strings . . . or

the hollow silence of before,
the echo of after?

Where does the music come from?

The not-so-pretty girl
with her flat feet in sensible shoes
pressing harmony into the floor,
sitting still as stone
with her shabby sweater
and uncombed hair
on the kitchen chair
in the corner of the room
alone . . . or

the listening?

14. Harpist. *Ceramic relief. Artist's collection.*

15. Hearing Angels. *Ceramic. Artist's collection.*

Hearing Angels

The woman who has been
lying on her side
rises up on an extended arm,
weight shifting forward
on the bow of her shining right shoulder
and her clenched right fist,
and stares deliberately,
without flinching or smiling,
into the middle distance.

Her left hand curls loose on her knee,
loose, too, hang her breasts,
while her buttocks and hips
and the long flexed left leg
are still heavy with her sleep.
The sockets of her eyes are deep
and the shadows gather in them
and in the deep lines around
her down-drawn waiting mouth.

But her spine twists twice,
arches back and pivots right,
with the tension
of her attention;
her hair twists, too,
coiled in a knot, like flight
from the nape of the rigid neck
that holds her head
sculpture-still
and awake.

She does not kneel;
there is no question
on her face.

Mary of Nazareth.
Joan of Arc.

Holy Communion

One of those long church days
sometime between the late afternoon
nursing home visit and the
evening deacons' meeting,
eating bag-supper alone at my desk,
no lamps lit against December sunset—
Connie phoned,
voice sharp in the darkness.
Bob was not home and she could not lift
Cathy from the dinner table
and get her ready for bed

and would I come?

I stood in front of the young woman,
hands under shoulders hollow as bird wing,
and, with her mother behind,
Cathy shifted her frail weight forward,
balanced to the bathroom
and sank into the hospital bed
someone had carried
over those narrow stairs.

16. Holy Communion. *Ceramic. Artist's collection.*

There was a wild-woman striped hat
on the bed frame.
The breast cancer support group
bought for each other
the most outlandish hats,
and then died, one by one,
in Boston hospitals—
died in their passionate hats.

Cathy understands the cancer.
She is a pharmacist.
She loves lilac-time and Christmas Eve,
and birthdays—especially
her daughter Carrie's
eight-year-old birthday.
Cathy used to make quilts and candles.
She traveled and had many friends.
She used to live
on Martha's Vineyard.

Now, in this Cape Ann winter twilight,
awkwardly supported
by her own mother and a minister
she met only a couple months ago,
she knew better than we
that she couldn't stand up,
even for Carrie,
against death much longer.

For Cathy now—it has come to
accepting help,
giving simple thanks for breath itself,
trying to smile and rest and
compose her face
for us
in lines of peace,
just one more Christmas—
for she will not see lilacs
or any new birthdays.

And as for me—back in the church
I took my bag-supper
into the nighttime sanctuary,
put the sandwich on the
communion table,
muttered a few words they teach
pastors to say,
and stood there in the dark

to cry on the bread.

California

madonna, woman of deep eyes
in another Nazareth,
the stories of your child
dwell in you already
because of your love.

The goat heavy-uddered
with milk tells of
languid simple days
of childhood.
The sun of warmth pours
grace-rays opening
a sky of baptism
long before the devil
or the dove.
The bark of terrier is
shrill with welcome
and warning
for some people will
hurry to his healing
and others will curl in
over the curse
they make of him.

There is labor in the fields—
the tired back
and lonely furrows
where only you
can see that seed
will come to grain.
Something of a parable
is in a mother's story.
And finally your heart
fingers the long road
that carves a traveling
down some miracles
and some betrayal
to a last meal
of grapes and tortilla
in some Pacific-washed
Jerusalem.

All the familiar stories,
the baby and the
mother's tears,
three trees on the horizon—
California nativity.

17. California Nativity. *Bronze. After "Born in a Carlsbad Canyon,"*
a song by Jerry Douglas Leggett. Artist's collection.

18. Execution. *Ceramic. Artist's collection.*

Execution

is like a priest being ordained
or a baby sleeping in a crib,
blowing sweet milky bubbles,
or a tired swimmer
stretched out
in sand on the beach
to let the sun warm
the muscles so ocean-cold.

Why else do we lie prone?

The teenaged girl
casts herself on the bed
for torrents of exciting love-tears,
the blanket-wrestler collapses
into the last posture of insomnia
an hour before dawn,
the child poses beside
a big-boned friendly yellow-dog
making believe
he has paws and haunches.

And then this—
the belly-down death,
this hand-tied submission,
so that the bullet buries deep
and without ricochet
into the ground,
and the soul lies flat and faceless,
so that grave-digging is easy,
and the executioner need not witness
any horrible jerking dance.

Hidden are the eyes,

and that is important because
no one who has become cruelty
could ever understand
the single precious moment in
execution
of feeling sand and pillows,
warm fur, cradle breath and
old holy stones,
for God is the embrace under.

19. Asia. Ceramic. Artist's collection.

Obituary

Official name: Preah Reach Ana Pak Kampuchea,
capital: Phnom Penh,
official language: Khmer,
official religion: Buddhism.

Birth rate: higher than the world's average,
death rate: higher than the world's average,
life expectancy: male, fifty-two years,
major causes of death: tuberculosis,
malaria, violence,
forgotten landmines, acts of war.

For every eight thousand people:
one doctor,
for every sixteen hundred people:
one telephone,
for every six people: one radio,
for all:
one newspaper.

And you are one kneeling man,
man of rice country,
sugarcane, cassava, timber country,
man of water buffalo country,
fishing, gemstone-smuggling country,
country of war.

Beloved husband of wife,
father of three girls
and two boys,
singer of Khmer songs,
literate, raiser of chickens,
eater of oranges,
of mangoes,
watcher of the nighttime sky for dawn,
while the smallest daughter
whimpers in a dream.

Around the radio
they will wait for you,
but you will not come home.

In the newspaper they will not
read your name.
Only in the official language of
statistics,
only in the official religion: the dead.

St. Francis

Lord,
make me a means
of your

open hands.

Where there is hatred let me sow

open smile.

Let me not so much
seek to be understood,
as to

open eyes,

to be comforted
as to

be still.

For it is in forgiving
that we are

face upturned,

and it is in dying that

we who are most foolish,
open and yet full
(hands, smile, eyes,
heart),

with our big ears and
fat lips and an Adam's apple bobbing
and rags for robes

and bare feet,
face,
and nothing hidden, not even
the God inside
are born, born . . .
we are born to everlasting life.

20. St. Francis. *Ceramic. Courtesy of Carol K. McCollough.*

21. Slave. Ceramic. Artist's collection.

Slave

Slave,
enslaved, slavery,
slavish, slaving,
enslavement,
Slave.

Subdue, subject,
subjugate, subordinate, dominate,
humiliate,
enthrall.

Submission, suppression, oppression,
bondage, servitude,
subservience,
chains.

Quelled, crushed, reduced,
shackled, bowed,
broken,
owned.

And this one—
collared, bent, twisted, captive,
naked, nameless,
Slave.

It is an infectious condition,
and only humans
are carriers—
this pestilence beyond words.
Plague.

Question . . .

Were you more than symbol-man—
boy of an African mother
playing in a Soweto township,
place of passport-fear,
of house arrest
and police brutality,
but home to a child?

Were you a young man in love,
ambitious and idealistic?

Did you work better
with your hands
or with your mind?
Did you go to the hills
for peace, or to the sea?

Did you dream that you
would become an old man
with big knuckles spread wide
on your knees,
the teller of stories,
one to go down to death
in earth of your own?

...Without Answer

The sculptor has made you
dead but not broken.
Smooth, still skin
forgets the hidden truth of
what happens to a body
beaten to death.
There should be
the marks of blows,
face swollen,
many shattered bones,
and muscles in spasm.
This, instead, is the relic
of your resting soul,
when nothing more
can be done to you.
This is the amen of you,
judging your killers.
For you are limp,
but they
have lost their lives.

And when the world
touches you,
Martyr,
miracles will happen.

22. Biko. Ceramic. Artist's collection.

Maybe

Reclining figure of
many women
drapes her arm across her eyes—
maybe they will not be open to nightmares
or even dreams,
maybe she will sleep the weary dayshift hours
before the graveyard of her cleaning
steel office towers,
maybe her children will not see her wake
and crawl all over her to play,
maybe she won't be hit,

maybe day rays won't dazzle a slumber
that only just began
after she steadied her querulous mother
one last time into the bathroom, or
after she heard her teenaged son
spin a dawnburst of gravel,
followed by the hollow thump of the car door
that must not be acknowledged, or
after she released her mind grip
from the job worry, or
the mortgage worry, or
the breast cancer worry, or
the pregnancy worry, or
after she looked over at the cold place
on the other side of the bed
and tucked her grief away.

Reclining figure
drapes her arm across her eyes
and all the maybe stories
wake and walk around
and tell each other
bedtime prayers.

23. Reclining Woman. *Ceramic. Artist's collection.*

24. Anger. *Ceramic. Artist's collection.*

Anger

"Anger"
    as a word
first appears in Middle English,
as it is derived from the
Old Norse—"sorrow."
The woman's stillness
casts a shadow—
that is anger.
It cannot be defined away.

She has the right to it—
you cannot take it.
You cannot extract its terrible teeth,
nor do you need to know
her reasons,
so that you can re-arrange them
into something acceptable,
or identify them
as right or wrong.
You may only know that
she has sat down
into a place
derived from old, old sorrow.

I respect her—I sit with her
until I am silent, too.
For anger is never abstract.
It is one woman,
and then another woman,
and then
another woman—
filled
with the broken stars.

The Old Fighter

Perhaps he is a prize fighter
or a freedom fighter,
in a long, long war,
or maybe a public defense lawyer
with heartbreak cases, and cases
he was afraid to win,
and never enough hours
or enough truth.

Perhaps he is an old doctor
with crow's-feet and heavy brows
telling too many people
their husband, wife,
child, parent is dying,
or maybe a farmer who struggles
to make a living from earth
so full of rocks
under a sky of sheer-sun
and rain at hay harvest.

Perhaps he is an old actor,
thinking about Lear, Prospero,
and too many commercials,
or maybe an old parole officer,
an old politician,
an old policeman,
an old union organizer
of coal miners.

Perhaps he is an old teacher,
watching the news
while some high school kid
(some kid in geometry)
gets pulled out of twisted metal
and broken glass,
or maybe an old fisherman
who has taken so many trips
out of Gloucester or Nantucket
that he knows just how
to look at wind
and the center of wind.

The old fighter is tired
with a tired that's been years coming
and he looks back on life
like a labyrinth—
no dead ends or shortcuts,
just many turnings,
a place that has a center—
like the wind or a prize ring.

And the old fighter is naked,

soul-naked, too,

because fighting is winning sometimes

and losing sometimes,

and it will always make you tired

and strip you bare,

and then, when you stop fighting,

you can look down

or back or inside,

and see you are a man.

25. Old Fighter. *Bronze.*
Artist's collection.

Valerie

She was a lot bigger than this when she died,
and slumped over,
and ten years older-looking,
and couldn't preach anymore
like she wanted to.

What was really big about
Valerie is that
she kept holding
that arm up
even when she couldn't.

26. Valerie. *Bonded bronze.*
Courtesy of Jerry Douglas Leggett
and Drenda Tigner.

She was a lot bigger when she died,
it made her friends angry
and cry,
but, Jesus, her eyes
would shine
right through you
with laughter
and justice like a fling of sunlight,
and she had this knowing
she must have
gotten on the other side of the stroke—

about black folks loving
and hurting, about anger
and joy,
and about how white folks
reserve a place
way down under the liberal
where they really don't expect
to be asked to change,

and about sitting courage,
and the Spirit talking
when the words don't
words don't
come out right—

because no big beautiful crazy
black woman
could know that much sweet shit about life
without breaking her heart.

Search

I am the searched one,
standing and defenseless,
with my dress and
my underwear
at my feet. I am the
strip-searched one
with my hands on my head,

but I am the searcher, too,
and you can keep your clothes
and your guns
and your jails.
I look through you
and I see nothing.

And beyond your nothing
I can see it purchased
at the price
of all that was human.
I continue to search
with my powerful gaze
for a truth
in the bone
you cannot hide from me.

There was once a child
sitting on his grandmother's lap,
eating red fruit
with much laughter—
the winter sun was warm
on his back.

A terrible price.

La Busqueda

Yo soy la buscada
parada y sin defensa,
con mi vestido y
mi ropa interior
a mis pies, yo soy la
despojada
con mis manos en la cabeza,

pero yo soy también la que busca,
y te puedes quedar con tus ropas
y tus rifles
y tus cárceles.
Yo miro a través de ti
y no veo nada.

Y después de la nada
puedo ver el precio
y el costo
de todo lo que era humano.
Yo sigo buscando
con mi poderosa mirada fija
por la verdad
en el hueso
que no puedes esconder de mi.

Habia una vez un niño
sentado en las piernas de su abuela,
comiéndose una fruta roja
con mucho gozo—
el sol invernal le calentaba
la espalda.

Que precio tan alto.

27. Search. *Ceramic. Artist's collection.*

Twisted Man and Twisted Woman

Twisted man and twisted woman—
he is twisted open and
she is twisted closed.
Is that the truth
molded in clay
and human figure
from some old
knowing about life
that the sculpture sees?

The man's arm is tensed
with hand clasped on foot.
And the contortions
of sharp angled
neck, shoulder, and knee
are bent to expose—
like the silhouette of a tree
gnarled by the wind
on a horizon of small hills.

28. Twisted Man. *Ceramic.*
Artist's collection.

The woman is twisted inward—
her head leaning on her knee,
her arms leg-embraced.
Her cross-hatched limbs
hide her open place
of birth, joy, pain.
Hers is a body woven,
a body made puzzle
and cave.

Horizon man, cave woman—
both human and body
and center.
Within the angled exposure,
and the folded hiding,
both are holy, long
before they are
twisted by life,

or seen by sculpture.

29. Twisted Woman.
Ceramic. Artist's collection.

A Small Remembering

Cry for the sisters of the broken bread.
Cry for the beaten prayers,
the vulnerable chapel,
the humble laughter
of women growing older.
Cry for the sabbath evening,
with candles of welcome,
wick-dimmed by tears.
Cry for the home of women where
still there are women who sing.

Pray for the sisters of the broken bread.
Pray for Edna Mary
and for Marie Julien,
gathered now in angel-wing,
comforted by quiet waters.
Pray for those who were deeply
wounded, for Mary Anna
and Patricia, pray that
as bruises darken and fade
their terror slowly heals.

Of blessed sacrament you were the
servant-sisters, and now,
you who kept vigil
have become the host.
Your cries and your prayers
are consecrated.
Your battered hospitality is holy,
and your pain and your death
are as sacred as the old pain
and the old spread-eagled
death of God.

Lift up your hearts.

We lift them up, and lift up
our broken bread—
in remembrance of you.

*[This poem is written for the women who
were attacked at the convent of the Servants
of the Blessed Sacrament in Waterville,
Maine, in January 1996, and for all
clergywomen and women religious who feel
the chill of fear within their commitment to
hospitality and yet do not bar their doors.]*

30. Nun. *Ceramic. Artist's collection.*

Orpheus

I ride the country of
shadow
between the living and the dead.
I hold the harp, the music
close to my breast—
and I feel the heartbeat
against the strings
of a song
I have not yet learned to sing.

I am not afraid to watch the
landscape
where human beings
tell stories of hope and fear.

 I am a myth—
you are my remembering.

31. Orpheus. *Ceramic relief. Artist's collection.*

Orpheus and Eurydice

Orpheus, son of the muse Calliope
and Apollo,
was born in Thrace
and became a musician.
He worshiped Dionysus;
he married Eurydice—
who was a dryad.

She was killed by a snake
fleeing Aristaeus.

Orpheus took his lyre beyond Styx
and played so
that Hades promised to
let them return to life
as long as Eurydice followed him
and he did not
look back.
There, you see,
is where the storytellers come in,
and the psychologists of men
and women.

He looked back and she went back.

Orpheus could not be consoled,
and so the Thracian women
tore him in pieces
and the Muses buried the broken parts
at the foot of Mount Olympus,
although his head came ashore
on the island of Lesbos
and there became a famous
oracle.

The mythology is about—
music and trust, fleeing and following,
burial, oracles, and hell.

The sculpture, which says even more,
is about fingers
and eyes.

32. Orpheus and Eurydice.
Ceramic relief. Artist's collection.

Unfinished Madonna

Mary naked

and she becomes
all women—
take away the veils
and the stars
in her hair,
and the clouds
and the manger,
even the sword
in her heart,
where the magnificat
is impaled
by the premonition
of cross—
and she becomes
a true icon
in which we mirror
how vulnerable
it is to nurse
God.

33. Unfinished Madonna. *Ceramic. Artist's collection.*

God,

who always

comes from

bodies and Spirit,

and lies in our

arms with only

our wisdom

between innocence

and slaughter—only

the woman-wisdom

that knows about

nakedness

because we have

sat down

both under the

snake-tree

and in the garden

where angels

walk and hail

our grace.

Eve

Long limbs I have,
and still face I have.
Rib, serpent,
fruit.
Fear-taste I have
in the leaf-cool of the day.

Cain-child I bear
and Abel-child I bear.
Death, question,
keeper.
Ground-soaked I bear,
more blood and more love.

34. Eve. Ceramic relief. Artist's collection.

The first woman I am,
and the first mother I am.
Named, naked,
covered.
A sword shines in the sunset
and an angel sings—

to me,
sweet clay and breath of God.

Escape-Women

Poised to run away,
bent forward and pausing,
she listens for the song—
sweet spiritual
in air that is thick with
summer heat, flowers,
and home-smells.
Southern green-land, goodbye.
Family, goodbye.
Nobody-troubles, goodbye.
She will follow the drinking gourd.
She will steal away to Jesus,
steal her own body,
steal away home.

Poised to run away,
eyes peer around edge of door,
she sees the red taillights
of his pickup truck,
pulling away
with all his anger—
words like blows,
and blows like blows—

stalking her soul
till she feels like dirt, spit.
She will follow the highway.
She will find a job or a friend,
throw her ring away,
kiss her pretty hand.

A hundred years between them,
a breath between them—
the women who escape.

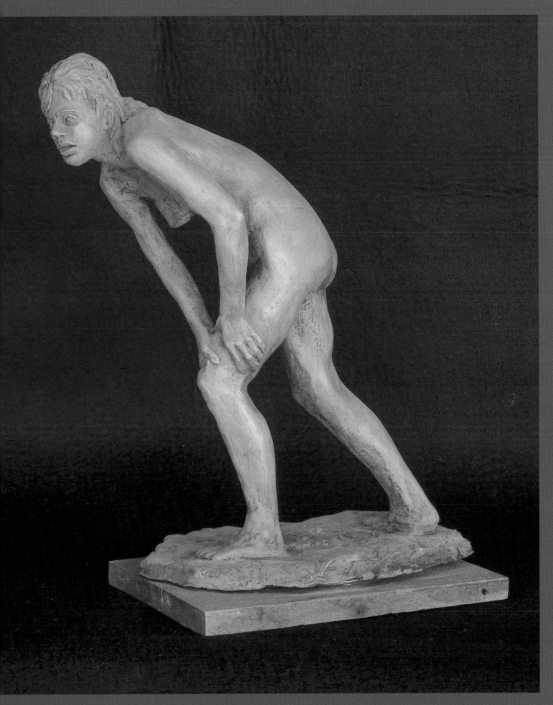

35. Escape-Women. *Ceramic. Artist's collection.*

Just Peace Award

Bronze circle, dove of peace,
reaching hand, broken chains—
waiting for new names
to fill you, to honor you—
new desmonds,
rosemarys, juanas, petes,
new nelsons and valeries,
new churches where
justice is so emmanuel
that God listens
to the preaching
in the lives.

Beautiful and vacant art,

scrap metal,

you are nothing but

the symbol of our faith

that there will always be

people who incarnate

the risky edge of gospel . . .

you are nothing but

the honesty of our despair

that the world will always be

crying out its need

for just such people

who struggle to keep

peace and justice alive.

Discus of thrown courage,

dish of the bread of life,

sundial of the time to act,

hubcap for crazy

old Ezekiel's wheel,

frisbee of the playful saints

and prophets, living

out their freedom lives,

face-relief of hope—

Just Peace Award.

Terra-cotta Crucifix

The shape of the terra-cotta man
fills the form of cross
so that barely a border
of execution
shows
and, for a fleeting moment,
it is the figure of a man
with outstretched arms,

as if the sculptor said—
this is about the One
whose bread-squandering,
demon-scaring, storm-stilling,
smelly life-raising,
profligate and messy love,
and revolutionary words
of equality
brought death upon himself.

Remember his bread
and words, his extravagant,
larger than life living!
Don't hide behind
the theological robes
of some bloody pornography
offered to a lip-licking god,
or the personal
sin-sponging isolation
of a revival tent,
or the lily-pretty funeral parlor
guarantee of eternal life.

Cruci—fix him
to the world!
Burst your heart with him!
Raise him—bony and offensive,
a barrel-chested, big-handed,
deep-eyed man, asking—
do you love me?
do you love me?
do you love me?
Then . . .

37. Crucifixion. Ceramic. Artist's collection.

Ode to Joy

I lean back to feel sunshine.
I bend up into some wonderful presence
that I cannot see,
but that radiates on my face
from without and within,
that resonates like the plucking
of cello string
in my dark wooden
music-making recess,
that remembers
God, or a new love, or the
unexpected happiness of a child.

I curl my toes
into some earth that is mine
because I've gone to the country
after a year of concrete,
or I own this farm
I thought would be foreclosed,
or I plant this garden of squash
and sweet peas and weed
and grow myself,
or just because I'm alive
after illness—
and dirt and rock

and sunshine—
have become the most profound,
the most unbelievably intense
and swiftly precious
hearts-unfold-like-flowers
opening . . .
symbols of my joy.

38. Joy. Ceramic. Artist's collection.

39. Candle Holders. *Ceramic. Courtesy of Christ Congregation, Princeton, New Jersey.*

Phalanges Candelabra

Hands holding candles,
   fine long-tapered piano fingers,
    curling around like tenderness,
    pointing you to flame
    and heaven.
    Christmas hands—
    hands that have touched
    straw and stars and
    frankincense.

   Hands holding candles,
    rough, big-knuckled hammer fists,
   gripping the light, guarding it,
 so it will never be
extinguished.
Emmaus hands—
hands that work and hurt,
know prayers and nails and
bread.

Hands, any hands—
   the claspers and clappers,
   the strokers and shakers,
    the wavers and writers and
    quilters and comforters
    of children—
    hands in use.

    Hands holding candles.

New Translation

"Suffer the little children"—
that was the old language,
and we used to giggle
in Sunday School
because, if we knew anything by heart
and not from the lesson plan
or the gold-star verse,
it was that this was a man
who wasn't just permitting
kids on the blessing lap
by sufferance,
as a mitzvah
or an obligation, but
because he liked to play,
to laugh, too, and

because he hoped that somehow,
if he spread his
big-fingered hand
around all that youngness,
it would radiate into him
the childhood he needed
to answer the long-faced ones—
the ones who pinch hours,
ration holiness,
prune tender shoots,
and, against the background
of all the adultly imaginative ways
to hate and hurt
that there have ever been,
push our mothers away.

40. Jesus and Children. *Ceramic. Artist's collection.*

41. Crucifix. *Wood. Artist's collection.*

Notes

FAITH AND GRACE, ART AND AWE

1. Maren Tirabassi reminded me that the reverse experience, learning of one's impending death, sometimes results in the same heightened awareness of the preciousness of life, of each moment, person, and place. Also, Kathleen Norris, another poet and well-known author of books such as *Dakota, Cloister Walk,* and *Amazing Grace,* names this sense of the preciousness of life as "gratitude," which she sees as "primary among spiritual virtues, the wellspring. . . . True gratitude is magnificat: that is, it magnifies. It refuses to remain strictly private but, like poetry itself, employs the personal to convey something more universal . . . reverberates throughout one's relationship with others and the world" ("Gratitude at Last," *Christian Century,* 3–10 June 1998, 582).

2. I owe the idea of "unexpected reprieve" to my friend Dr. J. Randall Nichols, professor at Princeton Theological Seminary.

3. Francis X. Clines, "28-Year Quest to Abolish Land Mines Pays Off for Veteran," *New York Times,* 3 December 1997.

4. One of the great advantages of sculpture is that people with sight disabilities can enjoy feeling sculpture with their hands. Sculpture is both a visual and a tactile art, even though touching is not permitted in museums. I encourage people, especially children and people without sight, to touch my work. I have also tried in this writing to use language about seeing and vision that does not exclude people without sight. My intent is to assume that all people have mental images that guide and stimulate their thought and that "seeing" a work of sculpture may require touching or recalling an image that may be out of sight for some.

THE VISUAL GOSPEL

1. I do not know Hebrew, so I asked for help from a scholar friend, Dr. Hugh White, professor of religion at Rutgers University. Three Hebrew words are important here: *pesel,* meaning a carved image such as one on a stone tablet ("graven" means carved); *masekah,* meaning a poured or molten image such as the golden calf; and *machshavah,* meaning a design, plan, skill, or work of

art. Bezalel was told to devise works of art, both carved (as in stone and wood) and poured (as in gold, silver, and bronze). There is no word for "idol" abstracted from real objects in the Hebrew Bible, according to White. So when a carved, graven image or a poured, molten image is made, there is the assumption that it will become an object of worship in the tradition of other contemporary religions. Such objects would then be false gods or idols because they were worshiped, not simply because they were made, thought, or imagined through the inspiration of God (i.e., "devised artistic designs"). Since such objects were so frequently worshiped, it was assumed that when such objects were found, the owner was worshiping them as idols (Judges 17:4). Clearly, the insult to God is the worshiping of carved or molten images instead of God, but not necessarily the making of such objects. According to White, the distinction between objects of art and idols awaited later linguistic and theological development.

2. The Second Commandment in Exodus 20:4 is translated "graven image" in the King James Version and the Revised Standard Version from the Hebrew *pesel*. However, the New Revised Standard Version (NRSV) freely translates it as "idol," presumably because that is the meaning of the negative command, not to worship any other gods than God. This distinction between an image (carved or poured, *pesel* or *masekah*) and an idol simply was not in the early Hebrew mental universe at that time, according to White. Since it is in ours and since that is the obvious meaning of the commandment, it makes sense for the NRSV to translate *pesel* as an idol we should not worship. It does not mean that thinking of or devising works of art (*machshavah*) is an evil act to be avoided. Indeed, with Bezalel, one can be inspired by God to make works of art for sacred places such as the tent of meeting.

3. It is helpful to reflect more on the difference between an image and an idol, for it is extreme. An idol (demon, Satan, obsession) points to itself, blinding its worshipers to slavish obedience to itself, closing the door to all but itself. An image points beyond itself, opening eyes like doors to see more than that image. An idol (e.g., drugs to a drug addict) takes over and controls a person's life, fatefully poisoning the soul with fear and hopelessness. An image merely signals a message that can bring new life and spiritual growth. An idol (demon, Satan, obsession) does not arise from one's own experience but invades one's soul from beyond itself. An image is a mental picture one constructs from one's own experience preceding that image. An idol originates elsewhere and enslaves the mind and perception. Instead of being controlled by an idol, leading us into spirals of fear and hopelessness, an image, as our mental construct that we control, can lead us to spiritual growth in courage and hope.

CREATIVITY

1. See the National Endowment for the Arts study of 1997, *American Canvas: An Arts Legacy for Our Communities* (Washington, D.C.: NEA, 1997), in which Gary O. Larson writes, "Sad to say, many American citizens fail to recognize the relevance of art to their lives. The product of an educational system that at best enshrined the arts as the province of elite cultures and at worst ignored the arts altogether, some people understandably view the arts as belonging to someone else" (p. 13).

2. Quoted in Rollo May, *The Courage to Create* (New York: W. W. Norton, 1975), 60.

3. For example, the Whitney Museum in New York featured an artist named Raphael Matanez Ortiz, who methodically destroyed a piano and other furniture with an ax and covered them with resin glue. These destroyed objects were on view as sculpture at the Whitney during the winter of 1997. Michael Kimmelman, the famed art critic for the *New York Times,* wrote about this show, "Today, we are dutifully informed in a Whitney brochure for the exhibition, Mr. Ortiz is regarded